Mackintosh to Mollino

FIFTY YEARS OF CHAIR DESIGN

Derek E. Ostergard

BARRY FRIEDMAN LTD.

26 East 82nd Street, New York, N.Y. 10028   (212) 794-8950

243 East 82nd Street, New York, N.Y. 10028   (212) 744-7240

PHOTOGRAPHY
Stuart Friedman, New York

DESIGN
Christopher Holme, New York

TYPESETTING
Stet-Shields, Inc., Stratford, Connecticut

PRINTING
Eastern Press, Inc., New Haven, Connecticut

FRONT COVER
Adapted from a detail of the back of Hill House chair
designed by Charles Rennie Mackintosh, 1904
(See catalogue entry No. 10)

BACK COVER
Adapted from the structural supports of armchair
designed by Carlo Mollino, 1949
(See catalogue entry No. 62)

CONTENTS

FOREWORD AND ACKNOWLEDGMENTS

Barry Friedman Ltd. is pleased to present its inaugural design exhibition, "Mackintosh to Mollino, Fifty Years of Chair Design." The success of our most recent painting exhibitions, "Fernand Khnopff and the Belgian Avant-garde" and "Tamara de Lempicka" provided the impetus for this comprehensive examination of twentieth-century chair design. Although the gallery has always shown nineteenth and twentieth-century European paintings and decorative arts, this represents our first presentation in the field of design.

The chair, perhaps more than any other single object, epitomizes the style of a given period. For that reason we have chosen to highlight chair design in our exhibition. The exhibit and catalogue provide the opportunity for the public to view important works by the most notable figures, such as Frank Lloyd Wright, Le Corbusier, Alvar Aalto, as well as work by such influential designers as Peter Behrens, Richard Riemerschmid, and Carlo Mollino. Their distinctive aesthetics, rarely seen in this country, played an important role in the formation of a modernist conscience. This exhibit also introduces the new annex to our gallery, where a portion of this show is housed. In the future, this space will display our collection of furniture, objects, and architectural drawings from this century.

Considerable resources were tapped to create a catalogue that is not merely descriptive but in many instances challenges established precepts. Several new dates, facts, and interpretations will, we hope, make this catalogue an invaluable aid. Although Barry Friedman Ltd. is a commercial gallery, our aim has always been to educate. Here we have proposed new answers to questions of design, societal influence, and artistic development. These topics are extensively discussed in the essay by Derek Ostergard which follows. With very keen interpretation, Mr. Ostergard analyzes the designer and his relationship to the world in which he functioned. Delving into social mores, economic changes, historic events, and artistic movements, the author provides unique interpretations of the evolution of design represented by the chairs in our collection. The essay is also complemented by an extensive bibliography which should be helpful to anyone studying chair design. Similarly, catalogue entries prove fresh and interesting though always carefully documented. We are pleased with the gallery's collaboration with such a scholar.

In an exhibition of this caliber, there are always many people who are involved in its assembly. For his continued help and expertise in many facets of this endeavor, I express great appreciation to Derek Ostergard. I would like to deeply thank my assistants, Jonathan Hallam and Debra Pesci, for their flawless research and organization, and, for his work on the bibliography, Gregory Gorrell. Much appreciation is also due to Stuart Friedman who almost exclusively handled the photography for this catalogue. Others who have contributed time and effort in making this exhibition a success should be recognized, namely, Christopher Wilk and Christian Witt-Dörring. I would also like to acknowledge the conservators who have aided in the continued preservation of these chairs; I extend my gratitude to Willie Gruenbaum for his care and handling of these precious pieces and to Dorothy Rudzki for sharing her extensive knowledge in the conservation of textiles. I am deeply grateful to the private collectors and institutions who have generously permitted their treasured objects to return once more to our gallery for public view. In particular I would like to mention the Metropolitan Museum of Art, the Carnegie Institute of Art, the Sydney and Frances Lewis Collection, and gallery Modernism. Their benevolence has expanded the scope of the exhibition.

Barry Friedman
New York, 1984

PERCEPTION IN EVOLUTION:
The Designer in Modern European Society

From the paternalistic figure of the nineteenth century to the activist of the twentieth, the progressive designer has been alternately viewed by society as both savior and subversive. No matter how mystical, humanistic, or practical his aspirations have been, the designer has been perceived in a mercurial fashion, often depending on the state of society at the time. Moreover, beyond his personally idiosyncratic behavior, the designer's own conception of his role in society has often placed him in a precarious position with critics, consumers, and representatives of the ruling establishment. As the designer has gained in confidence, he has expanded his role, particularly after the early years of this century, when he came to challenge the precepts he once upheld. Most importantly in alliance with the machine, the designer has been able to program his schemes on an international scale, investing his once anonymous role with a power only dreamed of by nineteenth-century figures such as William Morris.

By the time the Industrial Revolution was being hailed as the benefactor of the nineteenth-century European society, it was simultaneously generating a crisis of confidence in a world it had helped to create. Industrialization had suddenly created a need for concentrated pools of labor, bringing about monumental urbanization which fouled the environment, produced unprecedented poverty, and lowered the quality of life in general.

Nowhere was this situation more critical than in mid-nineteenth century England. First among nations to industrialize, it was also the first to suffer from unrestrained growth. As the workshop of the world, England flooded the international market with her mass-produced goods of inferior quality. This early inability to harness the machine was tangibly evident at the 1851 London Crystal Palace Exhibition where acres of manufactured products provoked a round of criticism heard well into the twentieth century.

The machine had introduced a disruptive element into the creative process whereby the craftsman was no longer solely responsible for the design and execution of his product. Now creation came most frequently through the combined efforts of a commercially motivated designer, an unskilled laborer, and a machine incapable of replicating the quality of handcrafted work. Within a decade of the Crystal Palace Exhibition, ideological reaction to this division of labor occurred.

As the first to suffer from industrialization, England was also the first to seek a cure. Concerned individuals such as William Morris, Ford Madox Brown, and Philip Webb felt that cultural regeneration could be effected through the transformation of the common man's environment. At a lecture delivered before the Leeds Philosophical and Literary Society, William Morris outlined his theory on the decline of quality in England and offered his plan for resolution:

> But I differ from some of those who are discontented with the present state of the arts in one important point: namely that they think that the matter is past hope and beyond remedy, whereas I believe that there is a remedy for the state of the arts which so arouses my discontent, and that remedy lies in improving the condition of those who produce or ought to produce art.[1]

The romantic quest for a return to pre-industrial values became the goal for the reformation of society. Essentially, Morris and his circle sought reform by trying to recapture the creativity and quality of a vanished agrarian society through the formation of a guild whose members would produce objects on an individual basis. Unlike their predecessors in the design world, however, they sought to serve a less advantaged clientele. Eventually, the popularity of their designs demanded an expansion of their small concern, and within a decade, Morris, Marshall, Faulkner and Company was transformed into considerably larger Morris and Company. In its new guise, the firm was responsible for the execution of complete interiors as well as individual items of furniture, stained glass, wallpapers, and carpeting. In order to meet demand, the machine eventually worked its way into their manufacturing procedure, and still the only clientele who could afford their services was a financially advantaged one. Morris' idealistic vision of elevating the existence of the common man through the efforts of the designer had been temporarily defeated. Nevertheless, through the legacy of his teachings, writings, and designs, Morris achieved a status of heroic proportions that inspired all succeeding generations. His resolution to introduce quality into the domestic scene was expanded in the twentieth century to include plans for reworking not only entire cityscapes, but societies as well. Morris, however, passed along one immutable concept to his successors — the designer's importance to society through his potential to improve the man-made environment.

During the final decades of the nineteenth century, the eyes of enlightened Europe were on the second generation of English designers who claimed inspirational and aesthetic descent from Morris. Richard Norman Shaw and C.F.A. Voysey were among those who continued Morris' pursuit of craftsman ideals in their progressive architectural essays. Specialty stores, craft guilds and design publications in England further emphasized the country's commitment to reform theory. Nevertheless, England's role in the twentieth century would be superseded by other European nations whose designers had been inspired by the paternalistic image England had established for their profession.

The technological benefits of the Industrial Revolution contributed to the sudden, but brief, flowering of a modern aesthetic in Scotland. The improved facility of rail travel and the increased accessibility of English design publications brought Scotland and particularly Glasgow, into close contact with the Arts and Crafts developments in England. By the late 1880's, progressive Scottish artists, architects, and artisans were emulating England's exploration of the regenerative powers of the past and the vernacular by promoting a local interest in Celtic history and their own traditions of the Stuart period. By the 1890's, this revival had provided an atmosphere conducive to the genius of Charles Rennie Mackintosh. But Mackintosh was not the only figure to contribute to the emergence of Glasgow as a momentary leader in international design circles. Surrounded by a coterie of similarly inspired artists and designers, he led them to an early acclaim which is evidenced by their contribution to an exhibition held in Liège in 1895. Local confirmation of

Mackintosh's talent came two years later. As a member of the respected architectural firm of Honeyman and Keppie, he was awarded the prestigious commission for the new Glasgow School of Art where he would develop his radical concepts in design throughout the next decade. Many of these ideas were applied to commercial establishments in Glasgow, as seen in a series of tea rooms Mackintosh designed for Miss Cranston. His highly personal form language, chromatic palette, and powerful disposition of interior spaces established Mackintosh as one of the first to work in a design idiom free from overt references to the past. As rapidly as his commissions confirmed his talent, however, his difficult and unpredictable behavior effectively destroyed his reputation, removing him from a position of influence both in Scotland and abroad. His sudden fall from favor was due to personal disfunction, not lack of design achievement. Nevertheless, Mackintosh, like William Morris, was highly inspirational as a designer. His work was especially applauded in Austria where "the presence of the Glasgow group in Vienna exerted a mainly psychological role."[2]

The foundations for the role of the indigenous designer in Austrian society were established before the turn of the century, largely through the efforts of Otto Wagner, a highly visible and respected figure in the Viennese community. Like many large European capitals of the time, Vienna had been rebuilt in the nineteenth century on a vast ceremonial scale, creating a need for engineered solutions to the ensuing anti-humanist environment of the city. Wagner's "polytechnical education [had] left him acutely aware of the technical and social realities of his epoch"[3], and his election to orchestrate the next stage of Vienna's development[4] underscores the faith that the reactionary imperial government and the conservative city fathers had in him.

As the architect of the establishment, Wagner deployed his considerable prestige to support the radical aims of the youthful Secessionists following their break with the repressive Academy. As mediator between Vienna's ossified past and promising future, Wagner became the role model for the designer as a viable and involved member of the modern community. He enhanced this image by publishing his *Moderne Architektur* in 1895. Enthusiastically received throughout Europe, the book was used by his students, including the prodigies Josef Hoffmann and Josef Maria Olbrich who absorbed his emphasis on the primacy of utility in design.

The remarkably short career of Olbrich is best remembered in context of the art colony he directed in Darmstadt under the patronage of the Grand Duke of Hesse, Ernst Ludwig, grandson of Queen Victoria. The duke's family ties had already brought the English Arts and Crafts designers Mackay Hugh Baillie Scott and Charles Robert Ashbee to Darmstadt. With Olbrich as his chief artistic advisor, the duke sought to elevate the quality of native arts and crafts so that his state would be more competitive in world markets. The evolving alliance between the designer and the state was acquiring commercial overtones. Yet after the art colony's monumental 1901 exhibition, *Ein Dokument Deutscher Kunst,* the organization floundered. This occurred partially because the personalities of high-ranking members of the community clashed, and also because the romantic goal of the colony was outmoded. Its anachronistic Arts and Crafts approach was economically unfeasible especially as other societies were losing their anxiety about the machine and its potential benefits.

In Vienna, the machine was well established by the late nineteenth century and had even acquired something of an anonymous benevolence. There, Michael Thonet's mass-produced furniture in bentwood had become a fixture in the cityscape as well as throughout the world. The aesthetic of this furniture, determined in part by the coordination of materials with the manufacturing process, permitted vast numbers of quality furnishings to be made at a low cost per unit. Wagner and his pupil, Hoffmann, also investigated the possibilities inherent in this material, and together with other members of the Viennese community, they irrevocably altered the nineteenth-century appearance of bentwood designs with a new geometric form language.

With the founding of the Wiener Werkstätte in 1903, Hoffmann became even better known for making his modernist designs available to an entirely different sector of society. From the smallest items of jewelry to entire residences, such as the opulent Palais Stoclet in Brussels, the guild garnered the attention of the establishment with custom-produced luxury goods executed in a progressive mode. Despite the scale of commissions, the guild retained a cohesive and idealistic approach to design.

> We wish to create an inner relationship linking public, designer and worker and we want to produce good and simple articles of everyday use. Our guiding principle is function, utility our first condition, and our strength must lie in good proportions and the proper treatment of material.[5]

Nineteenth-century Arts and Crafts principles, often linked with Hoffmann's distinctive aesthetic, lingered into the twentieth century in the Wiener Werkstätte until its termination due to economic hardship in 1932.

In Belgium, the indigenous designer attained an early preeminence by serving both the actual and symbolic needs of all strata of society. In 1900, the Belgian nation was comparatively new, created only seventy years before, after breaking from Dutch dominion. Throughout the nineteenth century, Belgium looked to Great Britain for its political security within the volatile European community. Unfortunately, it also emulated England's uncontrolled economic expansion which eventually made Belgium the most densely populated country in Europe, beset with severe political unrest. The vast wealth that poured in from the country's industrial base and its disproportionately large colonial empire created a new plutocracy overnight.[6] Unencumbered by a desire to emulate the reactionary habits of the aristocracy, a class that had never been strongly developed in Belgium, several leading industrialists selected Victor Horta to design their new town houses. Although remarkable for the use of industrial grade materials, transformed by Horta's dynamic creativity, these structures—symbols of their enlightenment, were only for the wealthy, seen by few and appreciated by fewer still.

Horta's early career produced one architectural achievement that received extensive public exposure. He brilliantly exploited his radical aesthetic in the Maison du Peuple, a multipurpose structure in Brussels designed for the Belgium Workers' Party. The selection of Horta to express the radical socialist aims of the powerful Belgium Workers' Party seemed the ideal synthesis of the designer, art and society. In the Maison du Peuple the designer was aligned with a specific cause involving the underprivileged of the twentieth century.

Henry Van de Velde also worked for the Belgian socialists – he was responsible for their graphic arts. His international influence at the turn of the century however, was considerably more effective than that of Horta's geographically confined work. Van de Velde's first major undertaking, his own residence at Uccle (1895), betrayed more than his own advantaged circumstances and distaste for contemporary design. In this structure and its furnishings, he revealed a debt to the English Arts and Crafts Movement as well as his future direction as an innovator in design. The Voysey-esque interiors of this youthful exercise were allied with reformist beliefs that the designer could improve the condition of man through a reworking of the environment.

Van de Velde soon applied this paternalistic notion to the mass-production of objects, all of which bore his unmistakable imprint. Discovered by the influential propagator of the French Art Nouveau movement, Samuel Bing, and the German art critic and historian Julius Meier-Graefe, Van de Velde rapidly rose to prominence. In Germany, through the patronage of Count Harry Kessler, Van de Velde received many commissions for private dwellings, designed a museum, as well as objects for production by various firms, and shaped the direction of the Weimar Art School and School of Arts and Crafts, which would be transformed into the Bauhaus in 1919.

One of the great determinants of twentieth-century design in Germany was the national mood of anxiety which gripped the nation in the late nineteenth century. Worried about its security as well as its arriviste image following unification in 1870, Germany pursued the "Iron and Blood" armament policy of Otto von Bismarck, the nation's powerful chancellor. His militaristic goal of German supremacy in Europe rested upon an economic stability, promoted by government. His policies helped to consolidate the nation's industrial base which had remained decentralized among the dozens of states that constituted Germany until the formation of the empire. Under the Hohenzollern dynasty, unbridled development became acceptable, with little consideration afforded the design of the manufactured item. As a result, "Made in Germany" became a perjorative term: a fact that heightened Germany's anxiety about its international image.

Why do we have to show the world that Germany's reputation for bad taste was well founded, because we have proved capable of reverting to the very style which revealed us bankrupt in London in 1851. Even if the limitations of 1850 are accepted at home, there is no doubt that they will have a disastrous effect on our reputation abroad.[7]

Official rectification began in 1896 when the German government dispatched Hermann Muthesius to London for four years to chart currents in British architecture and design with the hope of devising a national course of action. Individuals and private organizations in Germany also developed their own response to the deplorable state of design. During the late 1890's, Werkbunds, or guilds, were founded throughout the country. Under the creative direction of designers, these organizations produced furniture designs for independent manufacturers and furnishings for entire commissions; others were devoted to the development of a single discipline such as metalwork, glass, or ceramics. Frequently, these organizations had auxiliary training schools attached to them, which helped to train not only future artisans but designers as well. These schools sought a rapport between designer and factory, a rapport that would elevate the quality of manufactured goods.

The reworking of Germany's design community owed an inestimable debt to these Werkbunds. Suddenly the designer evolved from a minor figure in the community to a personage whose work would enhance the German image artistically and commercially throughout the world. Journalistic support for the progressive output of these Werk-bunds is evident: almost every German art and design publication highlighted this new work during this period, while devoting little space to historicist re-creations.

In 1907 the Deutscher Werkbund was created to humanistically "spread the realization among the German people that it is not only improper but outright stupid to execute work with one's hands only for the sake of appearance and without love."[8] Supported by almost every major design figure in Germany, including Hermann Muthesius, Richard Riemerschmid, and Peter Behrens, this society of designers, craftsmen, and manufacturers pursued many of the same goals as the smaller Werkbunds. Initially in this organization, the reform element was as personal in 1907 as it had been in Morris' time, nearly fifty years before. Under Muthesius' call for standardization in design, however, utilitarian and functional values were applied to industrial output.

In the same year as the founding of the Deutscher Werkbund, Peter Behrens was appointed chief designer to the monumental industrial combine Allgemeine Elektrizitäts Gesellschaft. There he would be responsible for the design of the company's buildings, graphics, and products. The search for an industrial *Gesamtkunstwerk* was in full effect with a unified industrial vision commensurate with the imperial might of the state.

What the undertaking ["Third German Arts and Crafts Exhibition" in Dresden] has in particular shown . . . is the fact that the latest efforts of industrial art are no longer merely the work of isolated groups of artists, but spring from roots whose ramifications have extended throughout the German Empire, and vigorous growth is the result.[9]

The interests of the German state as well as the output of German industry, now the responsibility of the designer, became more and more aligned. This remarkable phenomena is thought to be responsible, in part, for the revival of classicism in design and architecture in Germany before the First World War. Just as Percier and Fontaine had deployed the classical vocabulary to enforce the imperial aims of Napoleon, German designers borrowed from the same source to express the grandeur of the modern German state. That the linear nature of this vocabulary was more amenable to machine production than the more personal modes of design, made it all the more applaudable in the eyes of the Muthesius camp.

The iconography of an industrial empire was created through the work of her most noteworthy designers, who elevated its prestige in the eyes of the world. These progressive architects, in many respects the tools of the establishment, suffered following the devastation of World War I.

In contrast, France, perhaps the slowest major power in Western Europe to industrialize, turned to its past not only for aesthetic inspiration but for cultural affirmation as well. As Germany, Britain, and the United States aggressively jockeyed for dominion in the world marketplace with their industrially produced goods, France abdicated its position in this assembly of twentieth-century powers. The machine and its potential benefits for the French nations were not pressing concerns of the government. On the eve of the First World War, "the industrialization of France remained incomplete and left a large part of the economy in the grip of stagnation and stunted development."[10]

The French relied heavily upon the luxury trades for world recognition. The individual patron as opposed to the mass consumer remained important for French design in the early twentieth century, a lingering reminder of the aristocratic tradition of the eighteenth century. Perhaps more than any other professional, the designer would be responsible for maintaining the cherished, chauvinistic notion that France was the artistic epicenter of the world. The maintenance of this national notion was borne out in the signature products of La Belle Epoque.

Even with this focus, French designers of the Art Nouveau movement remained a loosely knit group of individualists with widely varying aesthetics. Hector Guimard, Eugene Gaillard, and Louis Majorelle, three of the leading figures of the movement, are no less valid as designers for the elitist audience they served than those who designed for mass production. Relying on traditional techniques of veneering and gilding as well as virtuostic carvings executed in exotic materials, they responded to predominently aesthetic considerations rather than to economic or manufacturing ones. Machinery was used, but rarely were designs overtly altered to accommodate the manufacturing process. Although their furniture was produced in numbers that might bring into question the meaning of "craft production," the most representative objects of these leading designers are those in which they responded to a rarified vision of the world. This unspoken endorsement of French traditions by the artist persisted until the Second World War.

Despite victory, France emerged from the First World War nearly ruined. Most of the battles had been fought on French soil; almost 1.4 million men were dead or missing, and countless were maimed. Unpaid war reparations destroyed the legendary stability of the franc.[11] Severely shaken by four years of war, this society sought refuge in the restoration of what Guimard and others adhered to in concept: the unassailable quality of French life and its tangible expression in the superbly wrought object.

Although prevalent modes of design in France changed drastically between 1900 and the 1920's, several spokesmen for French design did not. Maurice Dufrène and Paul Follot, youthful but influential figures at the turn of the century, were at the peak of their prestige in the years following the war. As highly eloquent figureheads, they represented continuity. Although historical assessment has not placed them in the vanguard of progressive design, one constant—that of premier quality—remained unquestioned in their work as well as others throughout the difficult 1920's. Modernists, in that their aesthetics were recognizably progressive, these designers continued to execute their work in traditional materials through the means of traditional techniques. During this period, the French government, more than ever, became a force in the design community, making the vast exhibitions of 1925, 1931, and 1937 less international showcases than vehicles for the display of national talents. The government's exclusion of the Germans from the 1925 exhibition was only one example of its protectionist policy. State patronage

of designers who upheld national values came in the form of commissions for embassies, museums, government offices and ocean-going vessels. Among those who worked in these government sanctioned modernist modes were such figures as Jacques-Emile Ruhlmann, Jules Leleu, and Eugene Printz. Economic factors during the 1930's would intensify government interaction with these designers and the subsidiary professions in the craft trades.

> On the eve of the Exhibition of 1937. . .a fear shared by the Government—that the divisions in France among designers would confuse the international public and harm sales of French decorative arts. Since so many artisans and small manufacturers were hard hit by the economic slump, the ideal for many French officials would be to silence the UAM[12] and the functionalists so that the dominant wood furniture styles would be given unanimous praise by visiting critics and journalists.[13]

For conservative France of the 1920's, the subversive designer came in the person of Charles Edouard Jeanneret, called Le Corbusier. Like Morris, Le Corbusier felt that man's lot in life could be considerably elevated by the work of the designer. But whereas much of Morris' work remained intimate in scale, to be specially used by individual consumers, Le Corbusier's was translated into a scale capable of serving vast sectors of the populace.

Many have thought that it was Le Corbusier's radical form language, devised from his unique synthesis of progressive materials and techniques, that alienated contemporary society. One must consider, however, the esteem in which Pierre Chareau and Robert Mallet-Stevens were held by the artistic community and government. Their work, designed in a mode similar to that of Le Corbusier, adhered to the deluxe standards of French tradition. In their almost unattainable luxury, the designs of Chareau and Mallet-Stevens were considerably beyond the means of the common man. Rather they updated the standards of the financially elite, while making them de rigueur for the established order.

Le Corbusier's aesthetic, initially introduced

through plans for individual dwellings, could easily be expanded into wholesale reworkings of the urban, national and international landscape. This transformation also dictated a complete alteration of accompanying cultural norms as well. His manifestos, propounded not only in his own journal but in international design competitions, earned him the reputation of a subversive. In a letter to the editors of the 1929 *Studio Yearbook,* Le Corbusier offered an ominous indication of the potential of his designs to transform society.

Will everything be completely changed? Yes, but, the state of architectural discord to which academicism has brought you (like everybody else) will be followed by a new condition of harmony. . .Cher Monsieur, believe me, we are inevitably in the threshold of a new architectural harmony.[14]

Finally, Le Corbusier's essential vehicle for achieving these plans, the machine, had lost a substantial portion of its prestige as a benefactor of society because of the monumental scale of devastation it had caused during the war. His image with bourgeois French society would remain questionable until after 1945.

In Germany, the designer suffered considerably as a result of the First World War. Suddenly, he became a figure of mistrust. As a tool of the pre-war and stridently nationalistic government, the designer lost credibility through guilt by association. Even Peter Behrens tried to absolve himself of much of his responsibility for the definition of the form of the pre-war industrial state, losing his preeminence after 1918.

The collapse of the Hohenzollern dynasty paved the way for a restructuring of society in Germany. No different from the French in their nostalgic longing for a time now gone, many Germans sought the forms and techniques of the past to achieve a vision of the present ultimately unresponsive to the post-war needs of society. Nevertheless, the reconciliation of art and industry that had been coordinated by the Deutscher Werkbund and others continued, but the preeminence of such organizations diminished considerably.

The figures who dominated design during the Weimar period (1919-1933) in Germany were members of a new generation that had often seen military action. The war left them with a profound distaste for the establishment and its shattering effects on society. Under the guidance of Walter Gropius, the Bauhaus, founded in 1919, would embody the progressive ideals of a young, enlightened Germany.

After that violent eruption, every thinking man felt the necessity for an intellectual change of front. Each in his own particular sphere of activity aspired to help in bridging the disastrous gulf between reality and idealism.[15]

The early years of the school were characterized by an intimate atmosphere, and a mystical, unconventional method of teaching introduced by a member of the faculty, Johannes Itten. In the anxious, early years of the Weimar Republic, Germans eager for a sense of normalcy found it difficult to view the school with anything but suspicion. The addition of foreigners to both staff and student body as well as the school's ties with the Dutch De Stijl movement and the Russian Constructivists heightened the anxiety of many Germans, paranoid about their position in the European community.

Political pressure forced the school to move from Weimar to Dessau in 1925-1926, after which it sought closer ties with industry as well as a more technological approach to design. The romantic vision of the school with its emphasis on the training of the craftsman was giving way to more pragmatic considerations: the school needed to prove its viability in relation to the growing needs of an impoverished society. The political activism of the students and the often expansive architectural schemes of its leaders, Walter Gropius and later Hannes Meyer, however, imperiled the school's reputation with the reactionary forces that gradually took control of the government by the late 1920's. The school was closed in 1933.

The varied design figures and schools of thought in the loosely grouped Scandinavian world, particularly in Finland, attained a sudden maturity in the years between the wars. Finland's independence from Russia in 1917 fostered a positive national attitude that affected all sectors of society.

The work of state agencies, industry, and individuals was characterized by a collective mentality rarely challenged by major special interest groups. By the time of independence, the Industrial Revolution had begun to affect Finland. Yet, neither the machine nor its relationship with society was elevated to the legendary status it had been in Germany, nor was it held responsible for a general disruption of society. The untapped potential of mechanization in Finland would be rapidly deployed during the 1920's and 1930's.

Alvar Aalto personified much of this growth in his own rapid evolution as a designer. Imbued with the national spirit, Aalto employed a vernacular mode and later an austere classicism to express his country's nationalist aspirations. It was his select absorption of various elements from progressive movements in both Russia and Western Europe, however, that established him as a figure of international repute by the early 1930's.

Under the benign patronage of industry, his exploitation of timber, his country's greatest natural resource, produced a distinct design mode, organic in its sythesis of program and materials. His work was critically identified as being nationally expressive: a fact underscored by the Finnish government's selection of his radical designs for their pavilions at the 1937 Paris Exposition and the 1939 New York World's Fair. These buildings were remarkable for their intimate spatial dynamics despite their large scale. His comprehensive projects, imbued with a humanistic concern for the psychological as well as the physical comfort of the individual, had a universal quality that easily translated to the international sector. Never viewed with mistrust, Aalto rarely incurred the opposition that his colleagues in Germany and France often had.

By the end of the Second World War, a large part of the enormous task of rebuilding countries often fell to the designer. As the unrecognized coordinator between governmental agencies and the private sector, the designer was viewed as an integral component of modern society. As a result of the monumental task of serving a burgeoning society, designers often adopted a specialized approach. Some became known for their work in home furnishings, others for architecture, and still others turned their attention to city planning. The aura of a Renaissance figure would no longer surround him as it had earlier in the century. Monumental responsibility had forced a concentration of his own efforts. No longer a luxury, the designer had become an essential component in society. This alteration of his role diluted the subversive characterization he received following the First World War, but also served to diminish the heroic stature the designer had attained in the nineteenth century.

[1] William Morris, "Art and Labor", *The Unpublished Lectures of William Morris,* ed. by Eugene D. LeMire (Detroit, Wayne State University Press, 1969), pp. 95-96.

[2] M.G. Messina, "Einfache Mobel", I "mobili semplici" di Hoffmann, *Hoffmann: i mobili semplici. Vienna 1900-1910,* ed. M. Fagiolo, ref. in "To the Limits of a Language: Wagner, Olbrich, Hoffmann," by Ezio Godoli, *Art Nouveau Architecture,* ed. by Frank Russell (New York, Rizzoli, 1979), p. 79.

[3] Kenneth Frampton, "The Sacred Spring: Wagner, Olbrich and Hoffmann, 1886-1912," *Modern Architecture: A Critical History* (New York, Oxford University Press, 1980), p. 79.

[4] For a detailed analysis of this phenomena in Vienna, see: Carl E. Schorske, "The Ringstrasse and the Birth of Urban Modernism," *Fin-De-Siecle Vienna, Politics and Culture* (New York, Alfred A. Knopf, 1980), pp. 24-115.

[5] Josef Hoffmann and Koloman Moser, "The Work-Programme of the Wiener Werkstätte," (1905), *Architecture and Design: 1890-1939,* ed. by Tim and Charlotte Benton with Dennis Sharp (New York, Whitney Library of Design, 1975), p. 36.

[6] Maurice Culot, "Art Nouveau Architecture in Belgium: Red Steel and Blue Aesthetic," *Art Nouveau: Belgium, France,* ed. by Yvonne Brunhammer et al. (Houston, Institute for the Arts, Rice University, 1975), p. 50.

[7] Hermann Muthesius, "Where Do We Stand?" (1911), *Architecture and Design: 1890-1939,* ed. by Tim and Charlotte Benton with Dennis Sharp (New York, Whitney Library of Design, 1975), p. 50.

8 Richard Riemerschmid quoted in Hans Wingler, *The Bauhaus: Weimar, Dessau, Berlin, Chicago* (Cambridge, M.I.T. Press, 1978), p. 2.

9 "Modern Decorative Art in Germany", *"The Studio" Yearbook of Decorative Art* (London, The Studio, 1907), p. 189.

10 Tom Kemp, *The French Economy, 1913-1939: The History of a Decline* (New York, St. Martin's Press, 1972), p. 25.

11 For a detailed account of the repercussions of the First World War on France see: J.P.T. Bury, *France, The Insecure Peace: From Versailles to the Great Depression* (London, MacDonald St. Giles House, 1972).

12 Union des Artistes Modernes, founded in 1930, was an organization of progressive designers in France devoted to the exploration of new materials and production techniques. The membership of this highly active organization included Francis Jourdain, Charlotte Perriand, Le Corbusier, Eileen Gray, Réné Herbst, Pierre Chareau, Jean Puiforcat, and Robert Mallet-Stevens.

13 Louis Cheronnet, from an article in *Art and Decoration*. Quoted from an article by Aaron Sheon, "Lucien Rollin, Architect-Decorateur of the 1930s: French Modern Furniture Design vs. German Functionalism," *Arts* 56 (May 1982), p. 115.

14 Le Corbusier, quoted from a letter to the editor in *The Yearbook of Decorative Art, 1929,* ed. by Shirley B. Wainwright with C. Geoffrey Holme (London, The Studio, 1929), p. 5.

15 Walter Gropius, "My Conception of the Bauhaus Idea," *50 Years Bauhaus* (Stuttgart, Württembergischer Kunstverein, 1968), p. 14.

Many people have generously contributed their support and knowledge to the assembling of this catalogue and exhibition. My deep appreciation goes to Barry Friedman whose first consideration in this endeavor was always the elevation of scholastic issues over those of a decidedly commercial nature. He never compromised with quality. Without the kind and truly dedicated support of the gallery's staff, Jonathan Hallam, Debra Pesci and Gregory Gorrell, the breadth of this catalogue would have been considerably reduced. Stuart Friedman's sensitive photography will enhance the reader's understanding of each entry. Dorothy Rudzki and Willie Gruenbaum employed their own considerable knowledge of their disciplines to aid in the presentation of the objects and the meticulous attention to detailed of editors Kathy Luhrs and Florian Stuber should be an example of all members of their profession. Angela D'Antuono supplied her charming disposition and critical facilities to the typing of this manuscript. Christopher Holme's superlative design for the catalogue was not completed with a deaf ear to our pleas for further extension of time.

Barry Harwood was instrumental in the pursuit of several evasive facts and Barbara Deisroth and Gerard Widdersoven generously helped us to locate an important object. Frederick Brandt of the Virginia Museum of Fine Arts was an enthusiastic supporter of the exhibition and Dr. Christian Witt-Dörring of the Angewandte Kunst Museum in Vienna always placed his cheerful and respected counsel at our disposal.

Finally, I would like to dedicate my work in this catalogue to Christopher Wilk of the Brooklyn Museum. His initial suggestion that I write the catalogue and his support thereafter, emphasizes that he is not only the most generous of colleagues but the most loyal of friends.

CATALOGUE OF THE EXHIBITION

Belgium
Side Chair, designed c. 1895
Made by the Société Van de Velde
Ash, upholstery
36½ x 18¾ x 18½ inches

A renaissance figure of towering influence in Belgium and Germany before the First World War, Van de Velde received much of his initial inspiration from English reform designers. Unlike the original Arts and Crafts figures, however, Van de Velde was rigorous in his advocacy of the machine and his rejection of historicism. This chair is similar to the model used in Van de Velde's own residence, Bloemenwarf, completed in 1895. The cut forms of the chair, with their buttress-like interaction, were executed by means of repetitive craft production, aided by machines.

Spain
Armchair, designed c. 1901-1904
Made for the Casa Calvet
Oak
38¼ x 26 x 20 inches

Designed for the Calvet family's private offices on the ground floor of their residence in Barcelona, this chair illustrates the vigorous manipulation of materials which characterizes Gaudi's work in both architecture and furnishings. Although the richly supple forms of the chair relate to South German or Italian Rococo designs of the mid-eighteenth century, the motifs are ultimately Gaudi's own, realized through superb craftsmanship.

France
Armchair, designed c. 1909-1910
Walnut, tooled leather
32¾ x 31 x 24 inches

The contrast between delicately
rendered detailing and robust form
creates a formal tension reminiscent of
work from the eighteenth century.
Guimard's distinctive abstract-organic
ornament, which defies historical
categorization, is perhaps the most
original used in France at that time.

Attributed to Gaillard
France
Side Chair, designed c. 1908
Mahogany, velvet upholstery
35 x 24¼ x 21⅞

The graceful proportions of the frame and the superbly carved details identify this chair as the product of a Parisian shop and most likely the design of Eugene Gaillard. Its distinct urbanity contrasts with the more vernacularly inspired forms of Art Nouveau, often characteristic of the school of Nancy. Here the free disposition of abstracted scroll forms appears to be Far Eastern in inspiration, borrowed perhaps from a Japanese print.

France
Armchair, designed 1900
Walnut, tooled leather upholstery
48 x 22½ x 30 inches

This forceful design is characteristic of Majorelle's work and of the school of Nancy in general. The massive frame is ideally suited to the bold detailing of the floral motif, itself inspired by the influential Emile Gallé, who advocated using nature as the ultimate design source. Enforcing this philosophy, Marjorelle has given the leather upholstery a tooled representation of a thistle (the symbol of the old province of Lorraine of which Nancy was the capital). Created in the seminal year of 1900, when Majorelle's creative powers and the Art Nouveau movement were at their peak, the chair illustrates the grandeur that this mode of design could attain.

6 Bugatti, Carlo (1856-1940)

Italy
Armchair, designed c. 1895
Mahogany, ebonized mahogany,
 inlaid with parchment,
brass, pewter ebony, leather
28¼ x 21¾ x 21¾ inches

Exoticism was a prevalent strain in
nineteenth-century high-style taste. It
is evidenced by structures, such as the
Brighton Pavilion in England, and in
the vast displays of foreign merchan-
dise exhibited at the large European
expositions. Bugatti, as heir to this
tradition, was highly creative in the
synthesis of sources in his designs.
The form of this chair, essentially
eighteenth century European in
inspiration, has been embellished
with a variety of motifs, alternately
identified as both Middle and Far
Eastern in origin. The extensive use of
inlay, repoussé, and contrasting
materials has produced a cohesive
design of bold originality.

Italy
Side Chair
Made for the artist's family
Mahogany, satinwood inlay, vellum
45 x 17⅞ x 20¾ inches
Mark: Table in set signed in ink "Bugatti"

Visually this design relates to Bugatti's
famous "snail chairs" used in his 1902
installation at the Turin Exhibition.
The snail chairs with their extended,
almost cantilevered seats were
designed for display and not necessar-
ily for practical use. In this particular
chair, Bugatti has alluded to the cantilever principle with even more vigor
than in the snail chair, but a medial
brace between the chair's rear
stretcher and seat rail provides the
essential load-bearing support. The
use of vellum here has introduced an
ethereal aspect to the design: its
translucency, unattainable with
conventional leathers and textiles,
imparts a luminosity to the delicately
colored designs rendered in watercolor
and crayon.

8 Mackintosh, Charles Rennie (1868-1928)

Scotland
Side Chair, designed 1897
Made for Luncheon Room at Miss Cranston's
Argyle Street Tea Rooms, Glasgow
Stained oak, rush
53¾ x 20 x 18⅜ inches

A series of these towering chairs around a table produced a semi-private enclosure within the larger public space of Miss Cranston's tea room. Given the generally diminutive stature of the Scotswomen who patronized this establishment at the turn of the century, the light passing through the pierce-work on the elliptical crest rails would have ideally imparted a halo-like glow about their heads. Without using the representational, druid-like imagery characteristic of his work in this period, Mackintosh endowed these commanding chairs with a mystical quality through the manipulation of form.

Scotland
Armchair, designed 1902
Three made: Two for Mrs. Rowat's house,
 14 Kingsborough Gardens, Glasgow,
 and one for artist's use
Painted oak, upholstery
45 x 27¾ x 22 inches

The articulated structure of this chair
and its attenuated lines illustrate the
mannerism that characterized Mackintosh's work from this period; so does
the starkness of the white paint, which
obscures the texture of the oak itself.
One of three examples of this model,
this chair was created for Mrs. Rowat
of Glasgow and exhibited in Moscow
in 1903.

Scotland
Side Chair, designed 1904
Two made: One for Hill House,
 Helensburgh [now in Glasgow Art
 Gallery], and one for artist's use
Ebonized oak, upholstery
40⅛ x 16 x 17 inches

The visual alignment of the lattice
motif up the back and beneath the
front seat rail visually minimizes the
bulk of this chair: an effect enhanced
by the ebonized finish on the entire
frame. Mackintosh retained dimension,
however, through the subtly curved
crest rail and rear stretcher, which
deviate from the abstract angularity
of the chair.

Belgium
Side Chair, designed c. 1901
Mahogany, upholstery
37⅝ x 18⅞ x 21⅞ inches

In designing his revolutionary interiors, Horta often exercised complete control over their furnishings. Although the construction and use of material was never as radical as in his buildings, his furniture was carefully coordinated with the architectural elements within a room. Here, the shaped crest rail bears a strong resemblance to the overdoors used throughout the Hôtel Solvay, a private residence in Brussels, for which this chair is reputed to have been made. According to Henry Hawley, a similar model was also used in the Hôtel Van Eetvelde in Brussels, c. 1897-1900.

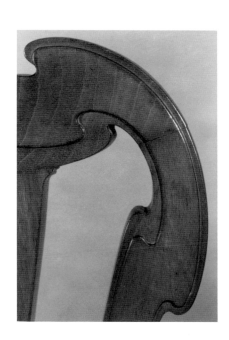

Born Moravia (now Czechoslovakia)
Armchair, designed 1898
Made for the children's room, Villa
Friedmann, Hinterbruhl, Austria
Walnut, upholstery
35 x 22½ x 20½ inches

In both the form and ornament of this chair, Olbrich reveals his predilection for the vernacular, the determinant of many of his early designs. A photograph of the chair *in situ* in the Villa Friedmann illustrates Olbrich's artistic search for the *Gesamtkunstwerk,* the total work of art. The form of a built-in cupboard/doorway in the children's room has been interpreted in the chair's stiles and side supports, which extend from the arms to the outer stretchers. In the year after the Friedmann commission, Olbrich became director of the Darmstadt Kunstlerkolonie, from where he affected much of the course of German design through the early years of this century.

Born Moravia (now Czechoslovakia)
Side Chair, designed c. 1900
Made by Josef Niedermoser, Vienna
Elm
36 x 18¾ x 19⅞ inches

This utility chair, designed for a bath-
room, first appeared in the German
publication *Das Interieur* in 1901. Its
simplified elements, with their
reliance on geometrical form,
illustrates the Secessionist vocabulary,
which Olbrich acquired while living in
Vienna in the 1890's.

14 Pankok, Bernard (1872-1943)

Germany
Side Chair, designed c. 1900
Made by Vereinigte Werkstätten
 für Kunst and Handwerk, München
American walnut, split cane
37⅞ x 21⅛ x 21⅜ inches

Here, the distinctive eccentricity and
angularity often found in Pankok's
more deluxe works have been
discarded for a classical language
evocative of the Biedermeier period.
The early nineteenth-century vocabulary has been augmented by Jugendstil
forms found in the cutwork of the
crest rail and in the tripartite segments
of the caned seat. Nevertheless, the
chair is part of the classical revival
that swept the German design
community following the decline of
Jugendstil popularity after 1900.

Germany
Side Chair, designed 1902
Oak, upholstery
38¾ x 17¾ x 18¼ inches

Behrens' training as a graphic
designer is revealed in the linear
definition of the components of this
chair. Nevertheless, sculptural qualities
have not been neglected, as seen in
the overlapping composition at the
intersection of the splat, stiles, and
crest rail. The arrangement of these
planar elements makes them appear to
be alternately advancing and receding.
This model appeared in a dining room
by Behrens shown at a 1902 exhibition
of modern interiors at the Wertheim
Department Store in Berlin.

Belgium
Side Chair, designed 1903
Made by H. Scheidemantel, Weimar
Oak, upholstery
37⅜ x 20⅛ x 21 inches

Early in this century, classicism became a predominant strain in the work
of progressive German designers. By
1903, even Van de Velde's work had
lost some of its distinctive Jugendstil
vitality; the sedate lines of this chair
contrast with much of his earlier
seating pieces. A reference to this
mode of design lingers nevertheless in
the ears of the paneled crest rail. This
model was used by Van de Velde in
the Nietzsche Archives in Weimar, the
city where Van de Velde executed
many of his important early commissions.

Germany
Armchair, designed 1901, model UW2545
Made by the Vereinigte Werkstätten
  für Kunst and Handwerk, München
Oak, upholstery
31 x 26 x 23¼ inches
Label: Stamped "2545", chalk mark on
  inside rear chair rail "2545"

An important design in Bruno Paul's
early repertoire, this model appeared
at the 1902 Turin Exhibition and at the
1904 St. Louis World's Fair, where the
German section generated great
interest among the progressive design
community in the United States.
Sculptural and graphic interplay has
been achieved in this chair through the
selection of materials. The oak grain of
the back panel hangs in a concave
swag formation, intersecting visually
with the convex crest rail of the tub
form.

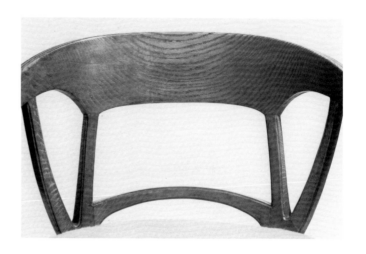

Germany
Side Chair, designed 1899
Made by the Vereinigten Werkstätten
 für Kunst and Handwerk, München
Oak, leather upholstery
31¾ x 21¾ x 22½ inches

One of the supreme achievements of
Jugendstil design, this chair appeared
at the Dresden Exhibition of 1899 and
at the Paris Universal Exposition in the
following year and was later retailed by
Liberty's Department Store in London.
Reimerschmid produced a remarkably
cohesive composition by gracefully
linking the upper rear stiles with the
lower forelegs. It is possible that this
linkage, used by several other
contemporary designers as well, was
inspired by Thonet's No. 51 side chair,
first manufactured between 1870 and
1880. As a member of the Munich
guild, Vereinigten Werkstätten für
Kunst and Handwerk, and as a founder
of the Deutsche Werkbund in 1907,
Riemerschmid was a prominent figure
in the German design community
before the First World War.

Germany
Armchair, designed c. 1900
Made by J. Fleischauer's Sohne, Nürnberg
Beechwood stained red
32⅜ x 22¼ x 20¾ inches

Historically descended from sixteenth-century caquetoire chairs, Riemerschmid's example also corresponds to George Walton's Scottish cottage chair used in his 1896 installation for Miss Cranston's Buchanan Street tea rooms in Glasgow. Riemerschmid's chair, however shows greater clarity of form in its cut and shaped back, which boldly defines the piece from the crest rail to the rear feet. This powerful element predates Frank Lloyd Wright's 1904 side chair (see catalogue entry 32) with its continuous back extending from the stretcher to the crest rail.

20 Riemerschmid, Richard (1868-1957)

Germany
Side Chair, designed c. 1903
Made by the Dresdener
 Werkstätten für Handwerkskunst, Dresden
Ash, leather upholstery
31¼ x 18¾ x 18⅞ inches

The distinct angularity of this small
chair gives it a powerful primordial
appearance which contrasts with the
prevailing classicism in other German
designs of the time. The shaping of
the individual elements reveals a subtle
visual and tactile sophistication
evidenced, for example, by the hidden
handhold beneath the crest rail.

Germany
Armchair, designed 1906-1907
Made by the Dresdener
 Werkstätten für Handwerkskunst, Dresden
Oak, upholstery
34½ x 25⅜ x 21½ inches

Designed by Riemerschmid as part of his *machinenmöbel programm,* a policy which advocated the use of the machine, this chair illustrates some of the spirit of his 1899 Dresden model, with its use of divided stiles. Yet the 1906 design has discarded of its predecessor's graceful elegance seen in the undisguised oak grain and bold articulation of form. The crisply rendered splats of the back and the paneled chair rails, delineated by machined screwheads, contrast with the handcrafted, sculptural treatment of the arms.

Austria
Armchair, designed c. 1899
Made by J. Bohn
Mahogany, leather upholstery, brass
30⅞ x 22¼ x 19⅞ inches

The extension of the sabots, like the glides used on furniture after the Second World War, allows a degree of mobility for such a substantial chair. The natural wood finish and lack of ornamentation mirror Loos' great anathema; tattooed or decorated architecture.

Austria
Armchair, designed 1902
Made for Austrian Postal Savings Bank, Vienna
Alternately manufactured by Thonet and J. & J. Kohn
Stained beechwood, plywood, aluminum
30⅜ x 22⅝ x 22⅝ inches

The use of simple bentwood furniture in the boardroom of Wagner's monumental Postal Savings Bank, testifies to the high esteem in which he held that material. Metal sabots and mounts protect the delicate finish, much as ormolu does on eighteenth-century furniture. That the metalwork is executed in aluminum is evidence of the architect's pursuit of a *Gesamtkunstwerk,* a cohesively designed environment. Aluminum elements are important visual and conceptual components of the building's interior and exterior detailing.

Austria
Armchair, designed 1902
Manufactured by J. & J. Kohn
Stained beechwood, plywood
31⅜ x 22 x 22⅞ inches

A variation of Wagner's Postal Savings
Bank chair (see entry 23), this model
more freely illustrates the geometric
vocabulary of the Secessionist school,
as seen in the circular perforations of
the back. By omitting the protective
aluminum sheathing used on the other
model, Wagner has made this chair a
purer expression of bentwood.

Austria
Armchair, designed c. 1902
Ebonized oak, leather upholstery
46¾ x 24¼ x 25¾ inches

Hoffmann has given bold and equal
definition to each structural element of
this chair while eliminating all references to historicism. The sled runners
extending beyond the rear legs lend a
monumentality to the chair which adds
to its architectural qualities. This motif
was also used in his designs for the
Spitzer and Wärndorfer commissions
of 1901-1902.

Austria
Side Chair, designed 1904
Made for the Purkersdorf Sanatorium
 by J. & J. Kohn
Beechwood, leather upholstery
38¾ x 17¾ 4 18⅛ inches
Label: Jacob & Josef Kohn, Wien

Although this chair appears in a 1906
Kohn catalogue, it was designed for
Hoffmann's Purkersdorf Sanatorium
near Vienna several years earlier. The
circle is the dominant motif in this
chair, which is executed two-
dimensionally in the splat and three-
dimensionally in the balls beneath the
chair rail. The circular form contrasts
with the stridently rectilinear treatment
of the building's interior.

Austria
Side Chair, designed c. 1906
Manufactured by J. & J. Kohn, Vienna
Stained beechwood, plywood
43½ x 17⅞ x 19⅝ inches
Label: Jacob & Joseph Kohn, Wein

One of the great enigmas of
twentieth-century design, this chair
has never been specifically
documented in a publication or
photograph of the period. Frequently
thought to be a variation of the
Purkersdorf Sanatorium chair, this
seven-ball chair is similar to a settee
that appears in a 1906 Kohn catalogue.
But the bold yet supple use of
bentwood in the back, which is
delineated by the accent balls, is so
characteristic of Hoffmann that it
strengthens the accepted ascription to
him.

Austria
Armchair, designed after 1907
Variation on the Cabaret Fledermaus
chair by J. & J. Kohn
Beechwood, plywood
28½ x 21½ x18½ inches

In this variation of Hoffmann's 1907
chair, the laminated saddle seat can be
said to be a precursor of Charles
Eames' shell forms of the 1940's.
Unlike the Eames work, however, the
complex curve is not an independently
stable form; rather, it relies upon a
raised seat rail and glue to maintain its
shape.

Austria
Rocking Chair, "Egg," designed 1905
Manufactured by J. & J. Kohn
Beechwood, split cane
47¼ x 21¼ x 42¼ inches

The most virtuosic of all bentwood designs, this rocking chair illustrates the great tensile strength of the material as well as its adaptability to the formal geometric language of the Secessionists. Purged of all ornament, the chair reveals the beauty inherent in structure alone. Several variations of this model exist, including some with adjustable back rests and others with leg rests that retract beneath the seat.

30 Schmidt, Wilhelm (1880-?)

Austria
Armchair, 1903
Made by the Prag-Rudnicker
 Korbfabrik, Vienna
Oak, split cane, brass screws
33 x 22 x 18½ inches

As a student of Joseph Hoffmann at the Kunstgewerbeschule in Vienna, Schmidt was a prominent member of the second generation of progressive Austrian designers to claim descent from Otto Wagner. Schmidt has instilled this chair with a distinct duality—an urbane design which contrasts with the rusticity of its materials.

Austria
Armchair, designed c. 1901-1903
Made by the Prag-Rudniker
 Korbwarenfabrik-Vienna
Maple, split cane, brass
30 x 23½ x 18 inches

The undisguised construction (see detail), bold expression of form, and simple materials of this chair relate to the contemporary work by Gustav Stickley in the United States and to designs retailed by Liberty and Company in London. The penetration of Arts and Crafts ideals into Eastern Europe is testimony not only to the power of the movement, but to the international dialogue between progressive designers at that time.

United States
Side Chair, 1904
Made for the Larkin Building, Buffalo
 and for the Artist's Oak Park
 residence/studio
Oak, leather upholstery
40⅛ x 15 x 18⅞

Until the Depression, tradition in the
United States dictated little exchange
of furnishings between the domestic
and commercial environments. Wright
defied that convention by using this
design in both the studio of his Oak
Park residence studio and in the Larkin
Building in Buffalo. The predominance
of the single plane of the back splat
lends this small chair a ceremonial
presence and may have influenced that
milestone of Holland's De Stijl
movement, Gerritt Rietveld's
"Red/Blue" chair of 1917/1918.

United States
Side Chair, designed 1907
Made by Charles Rohlfs
Oak, leather upholstery
36 x 17⅜ x 20¾ inches
Burned mark: R 1907

One of the boldest expressions of the
Arts and Crafts movement in the
United States, this chair, with its
reductivist form and rectilinear
elements, show how readily the
American adaptation of this initially
English school of thought translated
into machine production.

France
Armchair, designed c. 1913
Mahogany, split cane
31½ x 21⅞ x 19⅝ inches

Francis Jourdain, son of the nineteenth-century rationalist architect, Franz Jourdain, maintained reform ideals in France while most designers sought expression in more deluxe, historicist modes. A respected figure in the French design community, Jourdain exhibited this chair in his installation at the 1913 Salon d'Automne. His work following the First World War included numerous commissions from the government and public institutions, as well as collaborative efforts with other avant-garde figures.

France
Armchair, designed c. 1927
Made by Ruhlmann et Laurent for
 the Bloch Commission
Gilded beechwood, satin upholstery
40¾ x 30 x 31½ inches
Branded in wood: "Ruhlmann"

More than any other chair by
Ruhlmann, this design illustrates his
predilection for a historicist vocabulary
borrowed from the eighteenth and
early nineteenth centuries. From the
rectilinear treatment of its back to the
restrained line of its cabriole legs, the
chair alludes to a Régénce prototype.
The superb quality of the carving
strengthens this allusion. Ruhlmann's
own brand of mannerism eschews
pure revivalism as seen in the robust
proportions of the frame, which taper
into unusually small, scrolled feet.

France
Armchair, designed c. 1927
Beechwood frame, sycamore veneer,
 upholstery silverplated copper
31 x 28⅜ x 33 inches
Branded in wood: "PC"

Chareau, one of the founding
members of the radical design
coalition Union des Artistes Modernes,
is best remembered for his "Maison du
Verre," a private town house. He also
operated two retail establishments in
Paris—one on the Rue Nollet, the
other on the Rue Chez-Midi—where
furnishings designed by himself and
other prominent members of the
avant-garde community were sold.
This chair exhibits two major elements
of Chareau's distinctive aesthetic: the
use of pale colors and the riveting
delineation of form through angularity
of line. Similar chairs were used by
Chareau at his 1927 Beauvallon Golf
Club in Hyéres, the south of France.

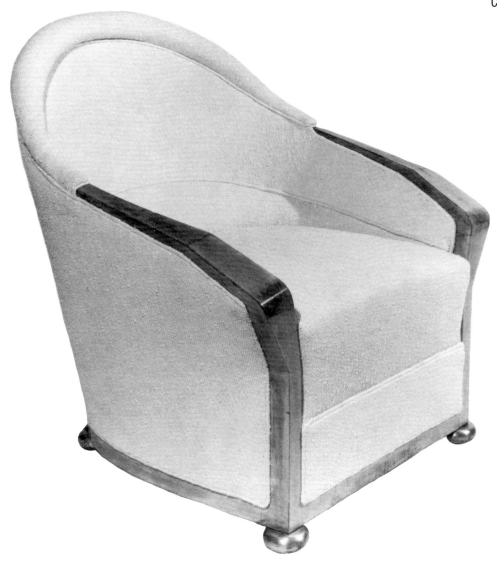

France
Armchair, designed c. 1932
Made by Chanaux & Company
Cerusé oak, pigskin upholstery
26 x 29½ x 30 inches
Stamped: Chanaux & Co.

Jean-Michel Frank's restrained palette
and his exploration of the decorative
qualities of material texture profoundly
affected many designers in the decade
before the Second World War. His
revolutionary elevation of straw, staff,
iron, and other lesser-grade materials
to a deluxe status earn him patronage
throughout Europe, South America,
and the United States. Here, oak, an
inexpensive wood, has been
indoctrinated into Frank's distinctive
aesthetic through the Céruse
technique. Powdered lead has been
forced into the quartered grain of the
wood to intensify its decorative
qualities. Adolphe Chanaux, a cabinet
maker, had alternately worked with
André Groult and Emile-Jacques
Ruhlmann, before joining Frank in the
late 1920's.

*38 Le Corbusier (1887-1965)
Jeanneret, Pierre (1887-1967)
Perriand, Charlotte (1903-)*

Switzerland
Switzerland
France
Armchair, "Basculant," designed 1928
Manufactured by Thonet
Chrome-plated, tubular steel, canvas
25½ x 25 x 26½ inches

The fauteuil "à dossier basculant" is
based on a nineteenth-century
prototype, the portable camp or safari
chair. Its light-weight components and
functional design provided inspiration
for several designers in the 1920's and
1930's. With the "chaise lounge" and
"sieges tournants," the "basculant"
contains moveable components, a
feature most German work in tubular
steel lacked at the time. This reference
to the machine, an important source
of Le Corbusier's iconography, is also
seen in the arms of the "basculant,"
which resemble conveyer belts.

Switzerland
Switzerland
France
Lounge chair [3-306], designed 1928
Manufactured by Thonet
Chrome-plated, tubular steel, matte
 black steel frame, calfskin fabric
26½ x 62½ x 19½ inches

The segmental cusp of the reclining
element and the parabolic form of the
legs reveal Le Corbusier's sensibilities
as a painter of the purist school.
Under the tutelage of Amedée
Ozenfant, Le Corbusier had learned to
emphasize the beauty inherent in
geometry and to respect clarity in
composition. The result of a collaborative effort of Le Corbusier's Rue de
Sèvres atelier, the chaise freely
exposes the dichotomy between "the
support" and "the supported" through
the use of contrasting materials.

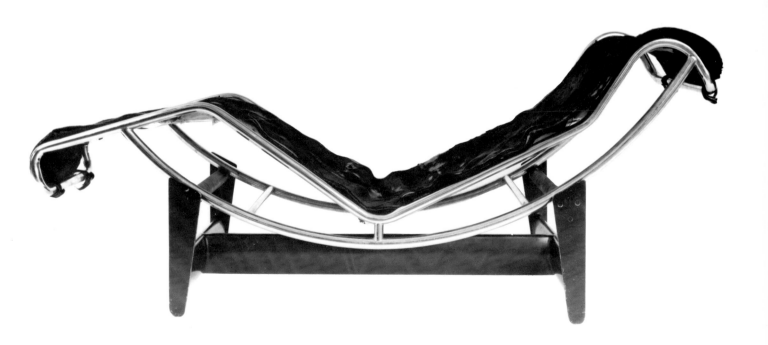

40 Breuer, Marcel (1902-1981)

Born Hungary
Armchair, "Wassilly" chair, designed 1925
Manufactured by Thonet
Nickel-plated steel painted black, canvas
29 x 32¼ x 29⅛ inches.

This prototype of the first tubular steel
chair was designed at the Bauhaus by
Breuer at the age of twenty-three. Its
acceptance by his peers and by the
large manufacturer Thonet helped to
dramatically alter concepts in
residential interior design: heretofore,
metal furniture had been acceptable
only in commercial and institutional
space, not in the domestic environment. This particular example is
reputed to have been in Robert Mallet-
Stevens' casino at Jean-de-Luz near
Biarritz. Although photographs do not
exist of this chair *in situ,* an article in
Art et Decoration in 1929 mentions the
French architect's use of tubular steel
furniture in the casino as well as
considerable work by Thonet Frères,
the French division of the Thonet firm.

Born Hungary
Armchair, (B34), designed c. 1929
Manufactured by Thonet
Nickeled steel, canvas
33¾ x 22½ x 26⅜ inches.

During the 1920's, the cantilevered chair suddenly became the attainable goal of many progressive European designers. According to Christopher Wilk, Mart Stam of Holland was the first to succeed with such a design in 1926-1927. Immediately thereafter, Breuer introduced his own model, the "B33" which marked the start of his extensive development of that theme. His superior handling of tubular steel produced the longest and most innovative body of designs, employing the cantilever principle.

Born Hungary
Armchair, (Model 301), designed 1933
Manufactured by Stylclair
Banded steel, painted plywood
29¼ x 22⅝ x 19⅞ inches.
Metal Label: Meubles Stylclair,
 License Wohnbedarf Lyon

Among progressive German architects of the 1920's, Mies Van der Rohe was the first to turn from tubular steel to explore design possibilities inherent in band steel. Examples of his experiments are the Barcelona chair and stool of 1929 and the Turgendhat and Brno chair variations of 1929-1931. Breuer followed this lead with his Wohnbedarf chair, which evolved from an earlier model he had designed in band aluminum (c. 1932-1933). The brittle nature of that light-weight material made it necessary for him to add structural supports beneath the rear of the seat, an addition here translated into steel. Such work in flat metal anticipates Breuer's later designs in flat sections of laminated wood.

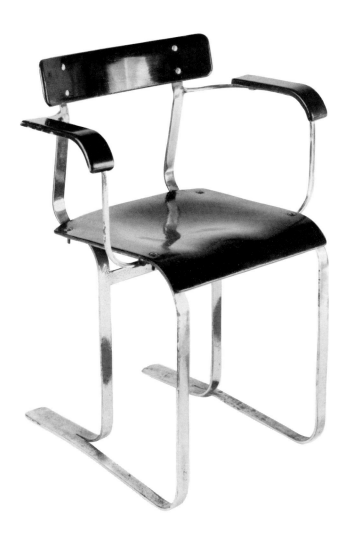

Sweden
Lounge, designed c. 1940
Manufactured by Karl Mathsson,
 Värnamo, Sweden
Plywood, solid birch, canvas
29¼ x 20½ x 59 inches

Son of a cabinetmaker, the young
Bruno Mathsson came to prominence
in international design circles in the
late 1930's with his elegant, fluid
designs employing solid and laminated
wood. Only the cradle base here is
made from laminates; the frame of the
reclining form has been achieved
through cut sections of solid wood
spliced together at the cusp and knee
supports in finger joints.

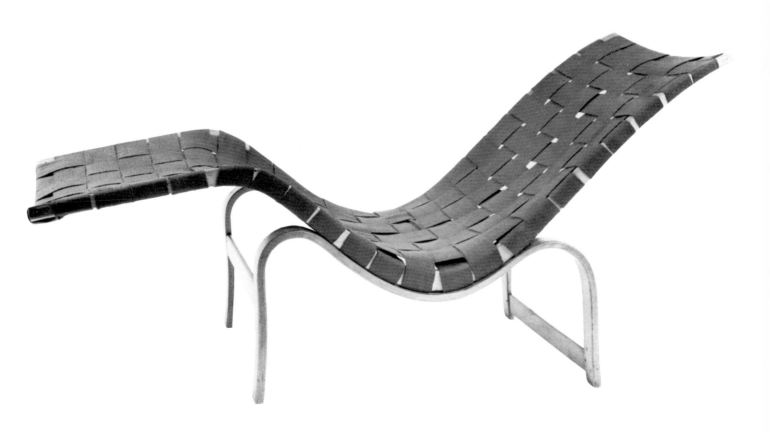

44 *B a u g n i e t , M a r c e l L o u i s (1 8 9 6 -   )*

Belgium
Armchair (adjustable), designed 1929
Chrome-plated steel, wood
 painted with lacquer, upholstery
36 x 20½ x 36⅜ inches

Between the World Wars, Marcel
Baugniet was a leader of the progressive design movement in Belgium. In
this reclining chair, he has updated a
nineteenth-century innovation, the
Morris chair, with a new form and new
materials.

Belgium
Lounge, designed c. 1935
Tubular steel, synthetic fabric
32 x 22½ x 53⅝ inches

The extension of the cantilevered back
of this chair illustrates the considerable tensile strength of tubular steel.
Its resilience offered not only seating
comfort but aesthetic possibilities
unavailable with any other material at
the time. Baugniet's design is similar
to a tubular steel chaise patented by
Breuer in Germany in 1932, which was
never produced.

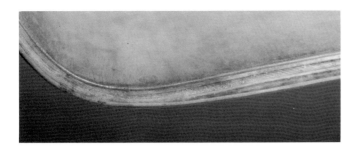

Finland
Armchair, "Scroll" chair, designed c. 1931-1932
Made for Paimio Sanatorium
Beechwood plywood, solid wood
25¾ x 23⅞ x 34⅝ inches

Although called the "Paimio" chair, this model was not placed into production until after Aalto's revolutionary Paimio Sanatorium was completed. This is not the first all plywood chair as commonly believed. Aalto's understanding of laminate technology, then in its infancy, is evident in the essential use of solid wood braces: two have been screwed beneath the scrolled form where it is mortised into the support frames, and a single rear stretcher joins the back. Unlike the work of his contemporaries, Aalto's bending of the wood form often involved the removal of several layers of the laminate (see detail).

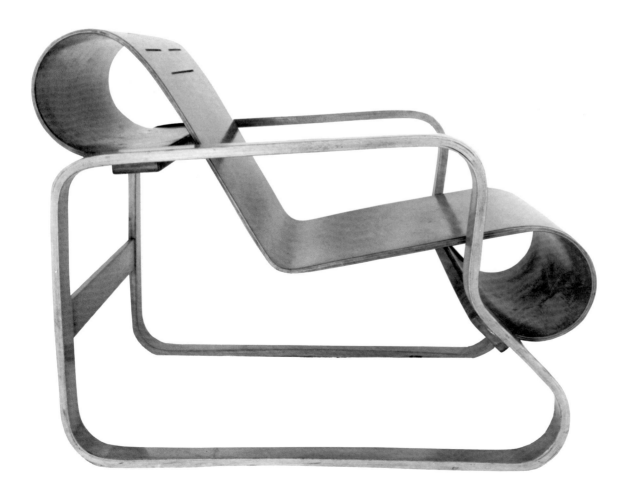

Finland
Armchair, "Spring Leaf," designed c. 1932
Manufactured by Stylclair
Distributed by Wohnbedarf
Plywood, solid wood
25¾ x 23¾ x 30 inches
Metal Label: Meubles Stylclair,
 License Wohnbedarf Lyon

Responding to German cantilevered
chairs in tubular steel of 1927-1928,
Aalto produced his own version with
a wood seat, around 1930, but its
support system was executed in
tubular metal. Technologies combining
special glues with beech laminates
allowed Aalto to extend his aesthetic
to the fullest with this model, the
first all-wood cantilevered chair which
was produced about 1936.

Great Britain
Armchair, designed c. 1934
Manufactured by Makers of
 Simple Furniture Ltd., London
Laminated birch
29⅜ x 23⅞ x 34⅞ inches.

As a designer of great creativity,
Gerald Summers remains an enigma
yet the chair he designed is recognized
as a major achievement in the development of the shell aesthetic. As the
first chair to be raised from a single
sheet of plywood, its construction
involved absolutely no assembly
process. This economical means of
manufacture allied with the light
weight of the product, which made it
inexpensive to ship, fails to explain
why great numbers of this chair were
not produced in the 1930's.

Great Britain
Side Chair, designed c. 1938
Manufactured by Makers of
 Simple Furniture Ltd., London
Laminated birch, upholstery
40½ x 17½ x 17½ inches.

The back of this chair gently expands
into a complex curve, following the
natural inclination of the wood grain to
seek release from the seat rail (see
detail) which binds the overall form.
One can view this chair as an inter-
mediary step between the simple
curve used in the Paimio chair of 1933
and the complex curve employed in
Eames' work of the 1940's. It remains
an important, if little remembered,
milestone in the development of the
shell aesthetic. Since the chair
appeared in the highly influential
Studio Yearbook of Decorative Art in
1938, it would have been known to
designers in Western Europe and the
United States.

50 Breuer, Marcel (1902-1981)

Born Hungary
Lounge, designed 1936
Made for Heal's Department Store, London
Sycamore plywood, upholstery
32¾ x 21 x 60 inches.

Designed by Breuer during his brief
stay in England in the mid-1930's, the
chaise is an interpretation of the
architect's earlier lounge chair for
Isokon. The use of cut-out sections of
plywood, used in the sides, would
dominate Breuer's furniture designs
during the late 1930's, particularly in
his work completed in the United
States.

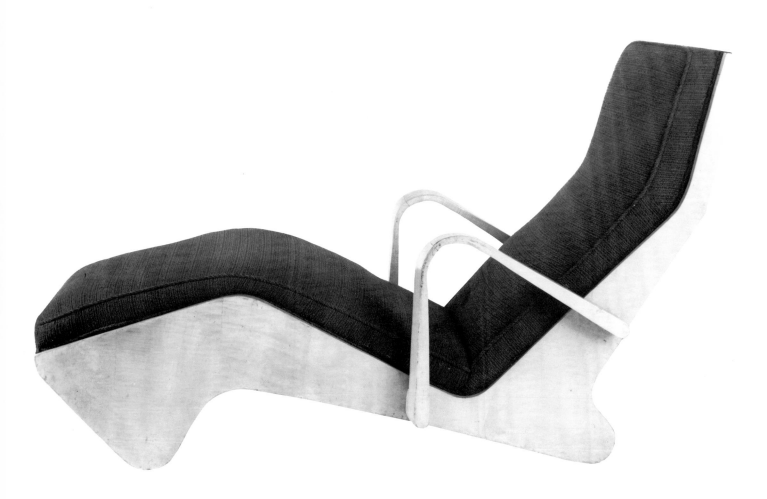

Born Hungary
Side Chair, designed 1936-1937
Manufactured by Isokon Furniture
 Company, London
Plywood
29¾ x 16 x 20¾ inches.

In terms of materials, this chair
completes almost a full circle for
Breuer who had turned from the
design of all-wood furniture in 1925 to
begin his revolutionary experiments
with tubular steel (see catalogue entry
40). When he later resumed his work
in wood, his earlier preference for
solid wood was supplanted by one for
laminates. Developed throughout the
late 1920's and 1930's, laminated wood
found favor with many progressive
designers of the period because of its
expressive potential and its suitability
for mass production.

United States
Side Chair, designed c. 1939
Lucite, wood, upholstery
33⅝ x 19¾ x 22 inches.

Remembered more for her personality and her arrangement of objects within established interiors, Elsie de Wolfe was responsible for one chair of distinction. Using a fanciful form evocative of Beidermeier designs of the early nineteenth century, she had this chair executed in the synthetic material Lucite, a product developed by DuPont in the 1930's.

United States
Side Chair, 1940-1941
Made for the Gregor Affleck House,
 Bloomfield Hills, Michigan
Cypress veneer, oak core
29¾ x 29 x 27 inches

The distinct planarity of this chair
looks back to Wright's earlier work for
the Larkin Building (see catalogue
entry 32). The use of the plane to
define form in Wright's later work, has
been frequently said to relate to his
interest in origami, the traditional
Japanese art of paper folding. The elements of this chair, as well as the
chair itself, were theoretically designed
to be cut and assembled by a
carpenter on the building site. The
plans for the Affleck House, a Usonian
structure, were exhibited at the
Museum of Modern Art in 1940.

54 Eames, Charles (1907-1978)
Eames, Ray Kaiser

United States
Chair, called "LCW" (Lounge Chair Wood),
  designed 1946
Manufactured by the Herman Miller
  Furniture Company
Plywood, rubber
26¼ x 22⅛ x 24¼ inches
Mark: "LCW" (incised), Herman Miller
  silver label

When compared to the Paimio chair of
1933, this chair of 1946 illustrates the
great strides made in wood technology
in little more than a decade. No longer
is the wood bent in a simple scroll
form; it has acquired a complex curve
that permits greater comfort in both
the seat and back. This innovation,
called the "shell," eliminated the need
for expensive upholstery without
sacrificing comfort. Eminently suitable
for mass-production, the shell
revolutionized the furniture industry
and established the Eameses as
leading figures in design.

United States (born Finland)
Armchair, "Womb 70," designed 1946
Manufactured by Knoll Associates
Plastic, latex foam, upholstery,
 chrome-plated steel
15¾ x 25 x 20½ inches.

Saarinen's first post-war design in the
shell aesthetic differs from the
Eameses work in the same mode (see
catalogue entry 54) in that the shell is
embellished by a foam and textile
covering. Saarinen's design also differs
from his former collaborator's in that
he has emphasized the separation of
the chair's elements through material
composition, texture, and color.

Denmark
Armchair, designed 1949
Manufactured by Johannes Hansen
Teak, split cane
30⅛ x 24¾ x 20¾ inches.
Metal label: "Johannes Hansen
  Copenhagen Denmark"

With its yoke back, bold form, and simple but impeccable joinery, this chair evokes early Chinese chairs, which Wegner could have seen in the collection of the Kunstindustrimuseum Museum in Copenhagen. The cane-work has been used to emphasize the graceful curve of the back, yet it is carefully and delicately patterned at the seat so that this element does not dominate the frame.

France
Side Chair, designed c. 1950
Manufactured by Jean Prouvé,
 Maxéville for the University
 of Strasbourg
Laminated wood, flat steel
34 x 20 x 27 inches.

Prouvé is a major figure in French
design, which has been characterized
throughout the twentieth century as
the final stronghold of the deluxe, one-
of-a-kind object. His lifelong work with
serial furniture identifies him as one of
his country's leading reform figures in
the past half-century, one who worked
against prevailing trends. As an architect, Prouvé has designed prefabri-
cated buildings, produced in response
to the housing shortage in France.

United States
Tub chair, "Coconut Chair," designed 1956
Manufactured by the Herman Miller
 Furniture Company
Painted steel, chromed steel, upholstery
32⅜ x 41¼ x 32½ inches

A dynamic tension is created through
the interplay of the seat and its
support system. The **V**-shaped
stretchers appear to be pulling the
immobile metal shell into its spherical
form, called "Coconut" because of its
resemblance to the fruit of the palm
tree.

United States
Armchair, "Swaged-Leg," designed 1956
Manufactured by the Herman Miller
  Furniture Company
Fiberglass, tubular steel
27⅝ x 28½ x 12 inches

Period analysis of Nelson's "swaged-leg" group ascribed his inspiration to the work of Eames, particularly the tub form of the chair and its electronically welded shock mounts. The gracefully delineated pedestal, however, deviates from many of Eames' leg systems of the early 1950's, which were more angularly articulated.

Italy
Side Chair, designed 1950
Made by Apelli, Turin
Plywood, upholstery
39 x 15¾ x 20⅜ inches

Here, minimal form has achieved
maximum comfort and distinctive
individual presence. Shaped brass
baffles define the independence of the
back element from the seating unit
without disturbing the cohesiveness of
the overall composition. Mollino's
masterful use of laminate technology
to express his own forceful aesthetic
remains unexcelled in the post-war
era.

Italy
Side Chair, designed c. 1952
Made by Apelli, Turin
Bleached oak, brass
36½ x 18¼ x 13¾ inches

Bipartite elements predominate in this chair, in the paired legs, splats, and crossbraces bolted through the back. Mollino enhanced this duplexity by having the seat and each splat executed out of two-wood sections apiece. Visually the chair relates to the laminated model by Mollino in this exhibition, but it differs radically in its construction. Rather than employ a laminate, Mollino had the chair cut, shaped, and assembled in a traditional manner.

62 *Mollino, Carlo (1905-1973)*

Italy
Armchair, designed 1949
Made by Cellerino, Turin
Bleached fruitwood, upholstery
40¼ x 22¼ x 22¼ inches

In Italy, the 1930's witnessed an
ideological division in design between
the Neo-classicists working for the
Facists, and the Rationalists, whose
output was related to progressive
developments in France and Germany.
Both groups, however, shared the
common denominator of austerity—the
Neo-classicist in design innovation,
the Rationalist in the range of materials
employed. Following the protracted
restrictions of a wartime economy,
a reactionary expression in design
occurred in some circles, particularly
in one which formed around Carlo
Mollino. His expansive work produced
a mode of Italian design, isolated
as Mollinian and identified as Baroque
in spirit. It found favor with a privileged
element in society, as evidenced by
its costly constructive techniques. This
remarkable armchair exemplifies the
flamboyance so characteristic of the
Turinese designer's work.

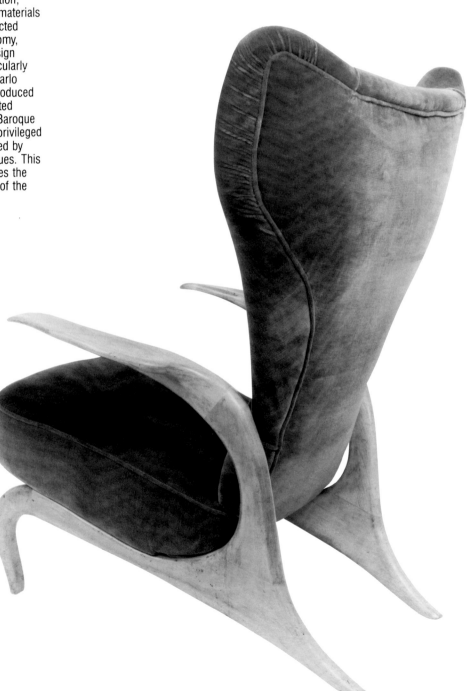

Italy
Lounge, "Rocking PS16," designed 1956
Manufactured by Carlo Poggi, Pavia
Birch, fruitwood, canvas
30⅞ x 27½ x 71¼ inches.

Albini worked in much the same
capacity as his better known contemporary Gio Ponti. As architect, designer
of furniture, and editor of magazine
Casa Bella, Albini exerted a powerful
influence in Italy. His installations of
interiors and furniture appeared in
numerous design exhibitions, including
the seminal Milan Triennale of 1936.
Here the rocking form of Le
Corbusier's lounge, without the
stabilizing cradle, has been translated
into wood and given a far greater
mobility.

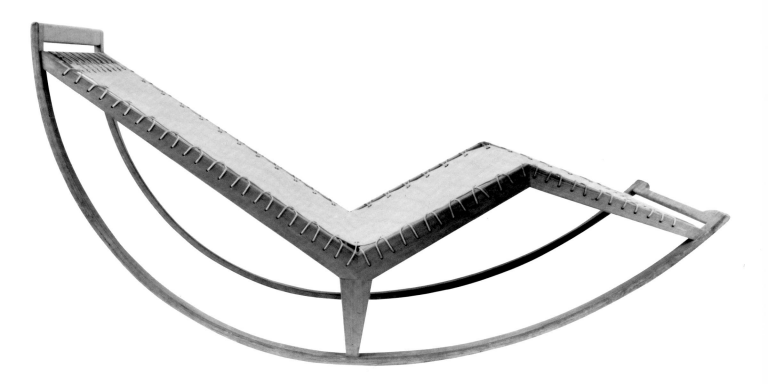

64 *J o h n s o n , D a n (dates unknown)*

United States
Dining Chair, "Gazelle" line, designed 1958
Manufactured by Dan Johnson Studio,
 Rome, for Arch Industries Inc.
Patinated bronze, split cane
33 x 19 x 18 inches

United States
Lounge Chair, "Gazelle" line,
 designed 1958
Manufactured by Dan Johnson Studio,
 Rome, for Arch Industries, Inc.
Walnut, split cane
36½ x 24½ x 33½ inches.

The sculptural quality found in so
many of Johnson's chairs is
emphasized by an advertisement
offering his "Gazelle" designs in either
wood, bronze, or aluminum. The
ectomorphic fluidity of the lines of
these chairs contrasts with the delicate
regularity of the canework. The
attentuated appearance of Johnson's
zoomorphic forms relate to the
mannerist work of Terrence Robsjohn-
Gibbings, employing a classical
vocabulary.

CHECKLIST FOR THE EXHIBITION

Labels and marks corresponding to the chairs used in the exhibition have been photographed wherever available and included in the checklist. However, this compilation of marks is not to be used as an infallible guide for those researching the marks and labels of designers and manufacturers of the twentieth century. For instance, it is known that Chanaux used different marks at different times of his career just as identical models of Van de Velde's chairs have been found marked and unmarked.

1. HENRY CLEMENT VAN DE VELDE
Belgium
Side Chair, designed c. 1895
Made by The Société Van De Velde
Ash, upholstery
36½ x 18¾ x 18½ inches

2. ANTONIO GAUDI (Y CORNET)
Spain
Armchair, designed c. 1901-1904
Made for the Casa Calvet, Barcelona
Oak
38¼ x 26 x 20 inches
Collection of Alan Stone

3. HECTOR GUIMARD
France
Armchair, designed c. 1909-1910
Walnut, tooled leather
32¾ x 31 x 24 inches

4. ATTRIBUTED TO EUGENE GAILLARD
France
Side Chair, designed c. 1908
Mahogany, velvet upholstery
35 x 24¼ x 21⅞ inches

5. LOUIS MAJORELLE
France
Armchair, designed 1900
Walnut, tooled leather upholstery
48 x 22½ x 30 inches

Lent by Museum of Art, Carnegie Institute, Pittsburg: Decorative Arts Purchase Fund, 1984

6. CARLO BUGATTI
Italy
Armchair, designed c. 1895
Mahogany, ebonized mahogany inlaid with parchment, brass, pewter ebony, leather
28¼ x 21¾ x 21¾ inches

7. CARLO BUGATTI
Italy
Side Chair
Made for use by the artist's family
Mahogany, satinwood inlay, vellum
45 x 17⅞ x 20¾ inches

8. CHARLES RENNIE MACKINTOSH
Scotland
Side Chair, designed 1897
Made for Luncheon Room at Miss Cranston's Argyle Street Tea Rooms, Glasgow
Stained oak, rush
53¾ x 20 x 18⅜ inches
Private Collection

9. CHARLES RENNIE MACKINTOSH
Scotland
Armchair, designed 1902
Made for Mrs. Rowat's House, Glasgow
Painted oak, upholstery
45 x 27¾ x 22 inches

10. CHARLES RENNIE MACKINTOSH
Scotland
Side Chair, designed 1904
Made for artist's use
Ebonized oak, upholstery
40⅛ x 16 x 17 inches

11. VICTOR HORTA
Belgium
Side Chair, designed c. 1901
Mahogany, upholstery
37⅝ x 18⅞ x 21⅞ inches

12. JOSEF MARIA OLBRICH
Born Moravia (now Czechoslovakia)
Armchair, designed 1898
Made for the Children's Room, Villa Friedmann, Hinterbruhl, Austria
Walnut, upholstery
35 x 22½ x 20½ inches
Lent by The Metropolitan Museum of Art, Friends of Twentieth Century Decorative Arts Gifts

13. JOSEF MARIA OLBRICH
Born Moravia (now Czechoslovakia)
Side Chair, designed c. 1900
Made by Josef Niedermoser, Vienna
Elm
36 x 18¾ x 19⅞ inches

14. BERNARD PANKOK
Germany
Side Chair, designed c. 1900
Made by Vereinigte Werkstätten für Kunst und Handwerk, München
American walnut, split cane
36⅞ x 21⅛ x 21⅜ inches

15. PETER BEHRENS
Germany
Side Chair, designed 1902
Oak, upholstery
38¾ x 17¾ x 18¼ inches
Collection of Sydney and Frances Lewis

16. HENRY CLEMENT VAN DE VELDE
Belgium
Side Chair, designed 1903
Made by H. Scheidemantel, Weimar
Oak, upholstery
37⅜ x 20⅛ x 21 inches

17. BRUNO PAUL
Germany

Armchair, designed 1901, Model
"UW2545"
Made by Vereinigte Werkstätten für
Kunst und Handwerk, München
Oak, upholstery
31 x 26 x 23¼ inches

18. RICHARD RIEMERSCHMID
Germany
Side Chair, designed 1899
Made by Vereinigten Werkstätten für
Kunst und Handwerk, München
Oak, leather upholstery
31¾ x 21¾ x 22½ inches
Collection of Sydney and Frances
Lewis

19. RICHARD RIEMERSCHMID
Germany
Armchair, designed 1900
Made by J. Fleischauer's Sohne,
Nürnberg
Beechwood, stained red
32⅜ x 22¼ x 20¾ inches

20. RICHARD RIEMERSCHMID
Germany
Side Chair, designed c. 1903
Made by the Dresdener Werkstätten
für Handwerkskunst, Dresden
Ash, leather upholstery
31¼ x 18¾ x 18⅞ inches

21. RICHARD RIEMERSCHMID
Germany
Armchair, designed 1906/07
Made by the Dresdener Werkstätten
für Handwerkskunst, Dresden
Oak, upholstery
34½ x 25¼ x 21⅜ inches

22. ADOLF LOOS
Austria
Armchair, designed c. 1899
Made by J. Bohn
Mahogany, leather, upholstery, brass
30⅞ x 22¼ x 19⅞ inches

23. OTTO KOLOMAN WAGNER
Austria
Armchair, designed 1902

Made for Austrian Postal Savings
Bank, Vienna
Alternately manufactured by Thonet &
J. & J. Kohn
Stained beechwood, plywood,
aluminum
30⅜ x 22⅝ x 22⅝ inches

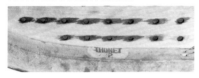

24. OTTO KOLOMAN WAGNER
Austria
Armchair, designed 1902
Manufactured by J. & J. Kohn
Stained beechwood, plywood
31⅜ x 22 x 23 inches

25. JOSEF HOFFMANN
Austria
Armchair, designed c. 1902
Ebonized oak, leather upholstery
46¾ x 25¼ x 25¾ inches

26. JOSEF HOFFMANN
Austria
Side Chair, designed 1904
Made for Purkersdorf Sanatorium by
J. & J. Kohn
Beechwood, leather upholstery
38¾ x 17¾ x 18⅛ inches

27. JOSEF HOFFMANN
Austria
Side Chair, designed c. 1906
Manufactured by J. & J. Kohn, Vienna
Stained beechwood, plywood
43⅜ x 17⅝ x 19⅝ inches

28. JOSEF HOFFMANN
Austria
Armchair, designed after 1907
Variation on the Cabaret Fledermaus
chair by J. & J. Kohn

Beechwood, plywood, upholstery
28½ x 21½ x 18⅜ inches

29. JOSEF HOFFMANN
Austria
Rocking Chair, designed 1905, "Egg"
Manufactured by J. & J. Kohn
Beechwood, split cane
47¼ x 21¼ x 42¼ inches
Collection of Miles Lourie

30. WILHELM SCHMIDT
Austria
Armchair, designed 1903
Made by the Prag-Rudniker
Korbwarenfabrik-Vienna
33 x 21¾ x 22⅛ inches

31. HANS VOLLMER
Austria
Armchair, designed c. 1901-1903
Made by the Prag-Rudniker
Korbwarenfabrik-Vienna
Maple, split cane, brass
30 x 23⅝ x 21 inches

32. FRANK LLOYD WRIGHT
United States
Side Chair, designed c. 1904
Larkin Building, Buffalo and artist's
Oak Park residence / studio
Oak, leather upholstery
40⅛ x 15 x 18⅞ inches

33. CHARLES ROHLFS
United States
Side Chair, designed 1907

Oak, leather upholstery
36 x 17⅜ x 20¾ inches

34. FRANCIS JOURDAIN
France
Armchair, designed c. 1913
Mahogany, split cane
31½ x 22⅜ x 19⅝ inches

35. EMILE-JACQUES RUHLMANN
France
Armchair, designed c. 1927
Made by Ruhlmann et Laurent for
  the Bloch Commission
Gilded beechwood, satin upholstery
40¾ x 30 x 31½ inches
Private collection

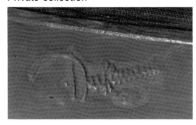

36. PIERRE CHAREAU
France
Armchair, designed c. 1927
Beechwood frame, sycamore veneer,
  silvered copper, upholstery
31 x 27¾ x 33⅛ inches

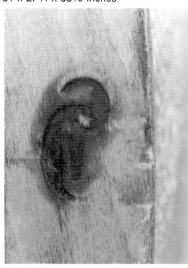

37. JEAN-MICHEL FRANK
France
Armchair, designed c.
Made by Chanaux & Company

Cerusé oak, pigskin upholstery
26¾ x 30 x 30 inches

38. LE CORBUSIER, Switzerland
PIERRE JEANNERET, Switzerland
CHARLOTTE PERRIAND, France
Armchair, designed 1928, "Basculant"
Manufactured by Thonet
Chrome plated tubular steel, canvas
25½ x 25 x 26½ inches

39. LE CORBUSIER, Switzerland
PIERRE JEANNERET, Switzerland
CHARLOTTE PERRIAND, France
Lounge Chair, designed 1928 [3-306]
Manufactured by Thonet
Chrome plated tubular steel, matte
  black steel frame, calfskin, fabric
26 x 63 x 21 inches

40. MARCEL BREUER
Born Hungary
Armchair, designed 1925, "Wassilly"
  chair
Manufactured by Thonet
Nickel-plated steel painted black,
  canvas
29 x 32¼ x 29⅛ inches

41. MARCEL BREUER
Born Hungary
Armchair, (B-34), designed c. 1929
Manufactured by Thonet
Nickeled steel, canvas
33¾ x 22½ x 26⅜ inches

42. MARCEL BREUER
Born Hungary
Armchair (Model 301), designed 1933
Manufactured by Stylclair
Banded steel, painted plywood
29¼ x 22⅝ x 19⅞ inches

43. BRUNO MATHSSON
Sweden
Lounge, designed c. 1940
Manufactured by Karl Mathsson,
  Värnamo
Plywood, solid birch, canvas
30 x 59 x 20 inches

44. MARCEL LOUIS BAUGNIET
Belgium
Armchair (adjustable), designed 1929
Chrome-plated steel, black-painted
  wood, upholstery
36 x 30½ x 36⅜ inches

45. MARCEL LOUIS BAUGNIET
Belgium
Lounge, designed c. 1935
Tubular steel, synthetic fabric
32 x 53⅝ x 22½ inches

46. ALVAR AALTO
Finland
Armchair, designed c. 1931-1932
"Scroll" or "Paimio" chair
Beechwood, plywood, solid wood
25¾ x 23⅞ x 34⅝ inches

47. ALVAR AALTO
Finland
Armchair, designed c. 1932, "Spring
  Leaf"
Manufactured by Stylclair
Distributed by Wohnbedarf
Plywood, solid wood
25¾ x 23¾ x 30 inches

48. GERALD SUMMERS
Great Britain
Armchair, designed c. 1934
Manufactured by Makers of Simple
  Furniture, Ltd., London
Laminated Birch
29⅜ x 23⅞ x 34⅞ inches

49. GERALD SUMMERS
Great Britain
Side Chair, designed c. 1938
Manufactured by Makers of Simple
  Furniture Ltd., London
Laminated birch, upholstery
40½ x 17½ x 17½ inches

50. MARCEL BREUER
Born Hungary
Lounge, designed 1936
Made for Heal's Department Store,
 London
Sycamore plywood, upholstery
32¾ x 60 x 21 inches

51. MARCEL BREUER
Born Hungary
Side Chair, designed 1936-1937
Manufactured by Isokon Furniture
 Company, London
Plywood
29¾ x 16 x 20¾ inches

52. ELSIE DE WOLFE
United States
Side Chair, designed c. 1939
Lucite, wood, upholstery
33⅝ x 19¾ x 22 inches

53. FRANK LLOYD WRIGHT
United States
Side Chair, designed 1940-1941
Made for the Gregor Affleck House,
 Bloomfield Hills, Michigan
Cypress veneer, oak core
29¾ x 29 x 26 inches

54. CHARLES EAMES
RAY KAISER EAMES
United States
Lounge, designed 1946
Manufactured by the Herman Miller
 Furniture Company, Grand Rapids
Plywood, rubber
26¼ x 22⅛ x 24¼ inches

55. EERO SAARINEN
United States (born Finland)
Armchair, designed 1946, "Womb 70"
Manufactured by Knoll Associates,
 New York
Plastic, latex foam, chrome plated
 steel, fabric
35½ x 39½ x 35⅞ inches

56. HANS WEGNER
Denmark
Armchair, designed 1949
Manufactured by Johannes Hansen,
 Copenhagen
Teak, split cane
30⅛ x 24¾ x 20¾ inches

57. JEAN PROUVÉ
France
Side Chair, designed c. 1950
Manufactured by Ateliers Jean Prouvé,
 Maxéville for the University of
 Strasbourg
Laminated beechwood, flat steel
34 x 20 x 27 inches

58. GEORGE NELSON
United States
Tub Chair, designed 1956,
 "Coconut Chair"
Manufactured by the Herman Miller
 Furniture Company, Grand Rapids
Chromed steel, painted steel,
 upholstery
32⅜ x 41¼ x 32½ inches

59. GEORGE NELSON
United States

Armchair, designed 1956,
 "Swaged-Leg"
Manufactured by the Herman Miller
 Furniture Company
Fiberglass, tubular steel
30 x 28⅝ x 22½ inches

60. CARLO MOLLINO
Italy
Side Chair, designed 1950
Made by Apelli, Turin
Plywood, upholstery, brass
39 x 16 x 20⅜ inches

61. CARLO MOLLINO
Italy
Side Chair, designed c. 1952
Made by Apelli, Turin
Bleached oak, brass
36½ x 18¼ x 18¾ inches

62. CARLO MOLLINO
Italy
Armchair, designed 1949
Made by Cellerino, Turin
Bleached fruitwood, upholstery
40 x 31½ x 32¼ inches

63. FRANCO ALBINI
Italy
Lounge, designed 1956,
 "Rocking PS 16"
Manufactured by Carlo Poggi, Pavia
Birch, fruitwood, canvas
30½ x 64 x 27½ inches

64. DAN JOHNSON
United States
Lounge Chair, designed 1958,
 "Gazelle" line
Manufactured by Dan Johnson Studio,
 Rome for Arch Industries Inc.
Walnut, split cane
36½ x 24½ x 33½ inches

65. DAN JOHNSON
United States
Dining Chair, designed 1958,
 "Gazelle" line
Manufactured by Dan Johnson Studio,
 Rome for Arch Industries Inc.
Patinated bronze, split cane
33 x 19 x 18 inches

BIBLIOGRAPHY

Books

Aalbers, Ben. *Stoelen,* Delft: Delft University Press, 1980.

Alison, Filippo. *Charles Rennie Mackintosh as a Designer of Chairs.* London: Academy Editions, 1978.

Ambasz, Emilio, ed. *Italy: The New Domestic Landscape.* New York: The Museum of Modern Art, 1972.

Behal, Vera J. *Möbel des Jugendstils.* Munich: Prestel-Verlag, 1981.

Benton, Tim and Charlotte, and Dennis Sharp. *Architecture and Design 1890-1939,* New York: Whitney Library of Design, 1975.

Billcliffe, Roger. *Charles Rennie Mackintosh: The Complete Furniture, Furniture Drawings and Interior Designs.* London: Lutterworth Press, 1979.

----------. *Mackintosh Watercolours.* London: Carter Nash Cameron, 1978.

Blake, Peter. *The Master Builders.* New York: Alfred A. Knopf, 1960.

Bonney, Thérèse and Louise. *Buying Antiques and Modern Furniture in Paris.* New York: Robert M. McBride & Company, 1929.

Bony, D'Anne. *Les Années 50.* Paris: Editions du Regard, 1982.

Borngräber, Christian. *Stil Novo Design in den 50er Jahren.* Frankfurt: Verlag Dieter Fricke, 1979.

Borsi, Franco and Paolo Portoghesi. *Victor Horta.* Brussels: Marc Vokaer, Editeur, 1977.

Branzi, Andrea. *Il Design Italiano Deglianni '50 a cura del Centrokappa,* 2 d ed. Milan:IGIS spa, 1981.

Brunet, César Martinelly. *Gaudi: His Life, His Theories, His Work.* Edited by Collins, George R., Cambridge, Mass.: M.I.T. Press, 1975.

Brunhammer, Yvonne. *Gaudi.* Paris: Musèe des Arts Decoratifs, 1971.

Burckhardt, Lucius, ed. *The Werkbund: History and Idealogy, 1907-1933.* Woodbury, N.Y.: Barron's, 1980.

Bury, J. P. T. *France: The Insecure Peace.* New York: American Heritage Press, 1972.

Cabban, Alfred. *A History of Modern France,* vol. 3. New York: Penguin Books, 1982.

Collins, George R., *Antonio Gaudi.* New York: George Brazillier, 1960.

Conrads, Ulrich, ed. *Programs and Manifestoes on 20th-Century Architecture.* Cambridge, Mass.: M.I.T. Press, 1970.

Cook, E. T. and Wedderburn, Alexander, eds. *The Works of John Ruskin,* Library Edition, vols. 1-39. London: George Allen, 1903-12.

Defour, Frans. *L'art du Meuble en Belgique au XXeme Siècle.* Tielt: Lannoo, 1979.

Dejean, Philippe. *Bugatti.* New York: Rizzoli International Publications, 1982.

Drexler, Arthur and Daniel, Greta. *Introduction to Twentieth-Century Design from the Collection of the Museum of Modern Art.* Garden City, N.Y.: Doubleday & Company, Inc., 1959.

Duncan, Alastair. *Art Nouveau Furniture.* New York: Clarkson N. Potter, 1982.

Dunster, David, ed. *Hector Guimard.* Architectural Monographs, 2. London: Academy Editions, 1978.

Faulkner, Peter. *Against the Age: An Introduction to William Morris.* London: George Allen & Unwin, 1980.

Fierens, Paul. *Marcel Baugniet.* Paris: Editions Marion, 1942.

Frampton, Kenneth. *Modern Architecture: A Critical History.* New York: Oxford University Press, 1980.

Geest, Jan van and Macel, Otakar. *Stühle aus Stahl.* Cologne: Verlag der Buchhandlung, 1980.

Geretsegger, Heinz. *Otto Wagner, 1841-1918.* Salzburg: Residenz Verlag, 1983.

Giedion, Sigfried. *Space, Time and Architecture,* 4th ed. Cambridge, Mass.: Harvard University Press, 1962.

Hanks, David A. *Innovative Furniture in America from 1800 to the Present.* New York: Horizon Press, 1981.

Heller, Erich. *The Artist's Journey into the Interior and Other Essays.* New York: Harcourt, Brace, Jovanovich, 1976.

Herbst, René. *Pierre Chareau.* Paris: Editions du Salon des Arts Ménagers, 1954.

Hitchcock, Henry-Russell. *Gaudi.* New York: Museum of Modern Art, 1957.

----------. *In the Nature of Materials, 1887-1941: The Buildings of Frank Lloyd Wright.* New York: Duell, Sloan and Pearce, 1942.

Howarth, Thomas. *Charles Rennie Mackintosh and the Modern Movement.* London: Routledge & Kegan Paul, 1977.

Kemp, Tom. *The French Economy, 1913-39.* New York: St. Martin's Press, 1972.

Larner, Gerald and Celia. *The Glasgow Style.* New York: Taplinger Publishing Co., 1979.

Latham, Ian. *Joseph Maria Olbrich.* London: Academy Editions, 1980.

Lemire, Eugene D. *The Unpublished Lectures of William Morris.* Detroit: Wayne State University Press, 1969.

Mannoni, Edith. *Meubles et Ensembles Style 1900.* Paris: Editions Charles Massin, 1968.

Mardaga, Pierre. *Adolf Loos.* Liége: Sole 'di-Liege, 1983.

Martin, J. L. *Circle.* London: Faber and Faber, 1971.

Massobrio, Giovanna. *La Seggiola di Vienna.* Turin: Martano editore.

Moussinac, Léon. *Francis Jourdain.* Geneva: Pierre Cailler, 1955.

Page, Marian. *Furniture Design by Architects.* New York: Watson-Guptill, 1983.

Pevsner, Nikolaus. *The Sources of Modern Architecture and Design.* New York: Frederick A. Praeger, 1968.

Popp, Dr. Joseph. *Bruno Paul.* Munich: Verlag von F. Bruckmann A. G., n.d.

Rasch, Bruder. *Material Konstruktion Form, 1926-1930.* Düsseldorf: Edition Marzona, 1981.

Rheims, Maurice. *The Flowering of Art Nouveau.* New York: Harry N. Abrams.

Richards, Charles R. *Art in Industry.* New York: William Edwin Rudge, 1922.

Rogers, Meyric R. *Italy at Work: Her Renaissance in Design Today.* Rome: Istituto Poligrafico dello Stato, 1950.

Roters, Eberhard. *Berlin, 1910-1933.* New York: Rizzoli, 1982.

Rubino, Luciano. *Pierre Chareau & Bernard Bijvoet dalla Francia dell'art deco verso un'architettura vera.* Rome: Edizioni Kappa, 1982.

Russell, Frank, ed. *Art Nouveau Architecture.* New York: Rizzoli International Publications, 1979.

Schnitzler, Arthur. *Vienna 1900: Games with Love and Death.* New York: Penguin Books, 1975.

Schorske, Carl E. *Fin-de-Siécle, Vienna.* New York: Alfred A. Knopf, 1979.

Sekler, Eduard F. *Josef Hoffmann.* Salzburg: Residenz Verlag, 1982.

Spencer, Robin. *The Aesthetic Movement.* London: Studio Vista, 1972.

Stein, Joseph, ed. *Bauhaus.* Cambridge, Mass.: M.I.T. Press, 1978.

Storrer, William Allin. *The Architecture of Frank Lloyd Wright,* 2nd ed., William Allin Storrer, 1978.

"Studio" Yearbook of Decorative Art, 50 vols., London and New York: The Studio, 1906-60/61.

Teirlinck, Herman. *Henry van de Velde.* Brussels: Editions et Ateliers d'Art Graphique Elsevier, 1959.

Tint, Herbert, *France Since 1918.* New York: St. Martin's Press, 1980.

Vivier, Robert. *Marcel Baugniet.* Paris: Les Écrivains Réunis, 1927.

Wichmann, Siegfried. *Jugendstil.* Munich: Schuler Verlagsgellschaft, 1977.

Wilk, Christopher. *Marcel Breuer: Furniture and Interiors.* New York: Museum of Modern Art, 1981.

----------. *Thonet: 150 Years of Furniture.* Woodbury, N.Y.: Barron's, 1980.

Windsor, Alan. *Peter Behrens: Architect and Designer, 1868-1940.* New York: Watson-Guptill Publications, 1981.

Wittlich, Petr. *Zeichnung aus der Epoche des Jugendstils.* Hanaum: Werner Dausien, 1974.

Catalogues

Archives D'Architecture Moderne, Brussels. *Rob Mallet-Stevens Architecte.* Brussels, 1980.

Arts Council of Great Britain in collaboration with the Victoria and Albert Museum. *Thirties: British Art and Design before the War.* London, 1980.

Brunhammer, Yvonne, et al. *Art Nouveau: Belgium, France.* Exhibition organized by the Institute for Arts, Rice University and the Art Institute of Chicago. Houston, 1976.

Contensou, Bernadett. *Leger and the Modern Spirit (1918-1931).* Musée d'art Moderne de la Ville de Paris. Paris, 1982.

Fischer Fine Art Limited, London. *Vienna: A Birthplace of 20th Century Design,* Vol. 1 (1900-1905): *Purism and Functionalism: "Konstruktiver Jugendstil"* London, 1981.

Forth Worth Art Museum. *Josef Hoffmann Design Classics.* Fort Worth, 1983.

Germanisches National Museum, Nuremberg. *Peter Behrens and Nürnberg.* Munich: Prestel-Verlag, 1980.

Glaeser, Ludwig. *Ludwig Miles van der Rohe.* Design Collection and the Mies van der Rohe Archive, Museum of Modern Art. New York, 1977.

Hahn, Peter and Wolsdorff, Christian, eds. *Bauhaus Archiv-Museum.* Berlin, 1981.

Herbst, René. *25 Années u.a.m.,* Salon des Arts Menagers. Paris, 1956.

Hessisches Landesmuseum, Darmstadt. *Ein Dokument Deutsches Kunst Darmstadt, 1901-1976* in *Kunst und Dekoration 1851-1914,* vol. 2. Darmstadt: Edward Roether Verlag, 1977.

Klaiber, Hans. *Bernard Pankok, 1872-1943.* Würtembergishen Landesmuseums. Stuttgart, 1973.

Kohn, Jacob & Josef. *Jacob & Josef Kohn der Katalog von 1916.* Munich: Verlag Dr. Graham Dry, 1980.

Küstlerhaus, Vienna. *Geborgenes Holz Konstruktive Entwarfe Wien, 1840-1910.* Vienna, 1979.

Liberty of London. *Liberty's 1875-1975.* London, 1975.

Moderne Vergangenheit, Wien, 1800-1900. Vienna, 1981.

Münchner Stadtmuseums, Technischen Universität, München, Germanishen Nationalmuseums Nürnberg. *Richard Riemerschmid, vom Jugendstil zum Werkbund: Werke und Dokumente.* Munich, 1982.

Musée des arts décoratifs, Paris. *Cinquantenaire de l'Exposition de 1925.* Paris, 1976.

Musée d'art Moderne de la Ville de Paris. *Leger et l'Esprit Moderne, 1918-1931.* Paris, 1982.

Museum Boymans van Beunigen, Rotterdam, *Jean Prouvé, Constructeur.* Delft: Delft University Press, 1981.

Österreicheshes Museum für Angewandte Kunst, Vienna. *Die Wiener Werkstätte Modernes Kunsthandwerk von 1903-1932.* Vienna, 1967.

Palais des Beaux-Arts, Brussels. *Henry van de Velde, 1863-1957.* Brussels, 1963.

Puolo, Maurizio D. *Le Corbusier, Charlotte Perriaud, Pierre Jeanneret.* Mostra al Palazzo dei Convegni. Rome: De Luca Editore, 1976.

Richter, Wolfgang. *Josef Hoffmann und Sein Kreis Möbel, 1900-1930.* Galerie Alt Wien. Munich, 1980.

Royal Academy, London. *Bauhaus—50 Years.* London, 1964.

Société des Expositions Palais des Beaux-Arts, Brussels. *Art Nouveau Belgique.* Brussels, 1980-81.

Victoria and Albert Museum, London. *Modern Chairs, 1918-1970.* An interna-

tional exhibition presented by the White-
chapel Art Gallery in association with
the Observer. London, 1970.

Periodicals

Art et Decoration. Editions Albert Levy.
Paris, (1897-1938).

Deutsche Kunst and Dekoration.
(1897-1934) Darmstadt, Alexander H.
Koch.

Feuillets d'art. Paris 1919-1922.

Henri Van de Velde Theatres, 1904-1914.
An Architectural Association Quarterly.
(The Architectural Association London/
Archives de l'Architecture Moderne,
Bruxelles), (1974).

Innen-dekoration. Darmstadt, (1890-1939).

Das Interieur Kunstverlag Anton Schroll &
Co., Wien, (1900-1904).

Kunst and Kunsthandwerk. Osterreich-
ishces Museum für Kunst and industrie.
Wien, (1891-1921).

Mobilier et Décoration. Éditions Mobilier
et Décoration. Sèvres 1931 to date.

Moderne Bauformen. Julius Hoffman,
Stuttgart, 1902-1944.

Monastshefte für Baukunst. Wasmuth,
Berlin, 1902-1944.

Renaissance d'Art. Paris, (1918-1939).

Revue de l'art ancien et moderne. Paris,
(1897-1937).

Sheon, Aaron. "Lucien Rollin, Architecte-
Decorateur of the 1930's: French Modern
Furniture Design vs. German Functionalism", *Arts Magazine*. 56 No. 9 (May
1982), 104-118.

Vogue. Conde Nast, New York,
(1919-1939).

Wendingen. H. Th. Wijdeveld, Amsterdam,
(1918-1931).